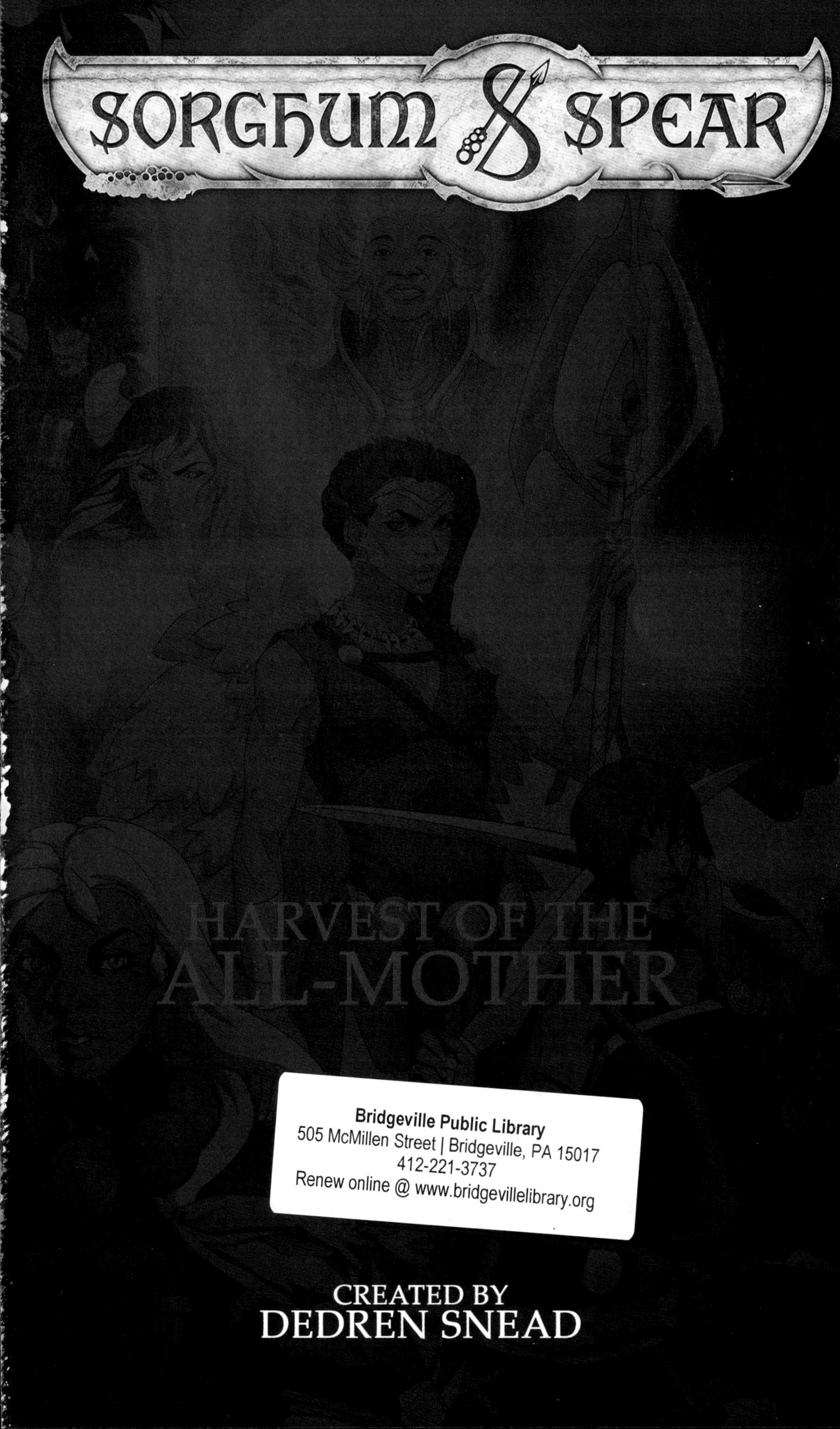
SORGHUM & SPEAR
HARVEST OF THE
ALL-MOTHER
CREATED BY
DEDREN SNEAD

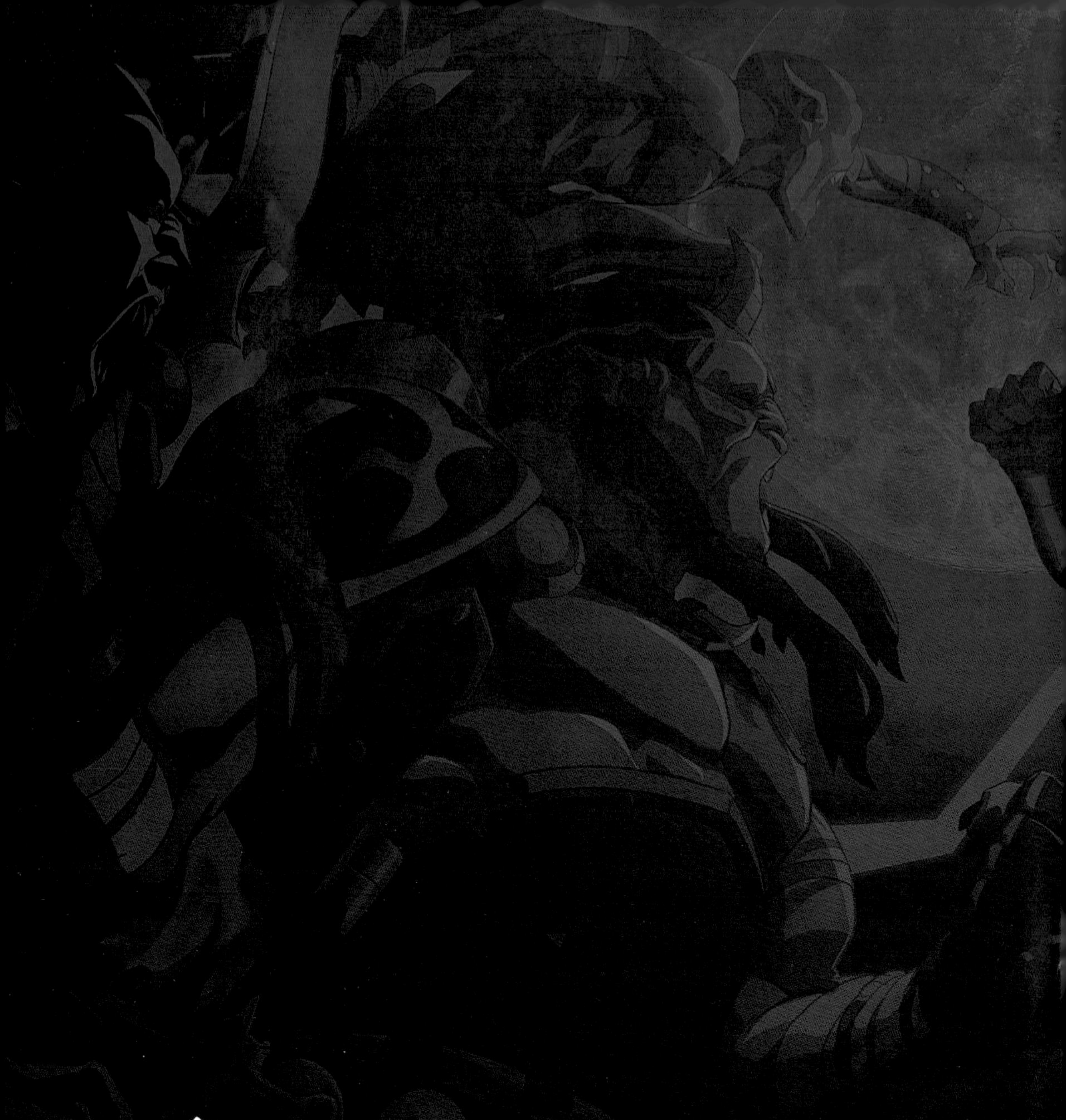

OUTLAND ENTERTAINMENT

Jeremy D. Mohler
Publisher & Creative Director
Alana Joli Abbot
Editor in Chief

3119 Gillham Road
Kansas City MO, 64109
P. 785.640.4324
Email. jeremy@outlandentertainment.com

WWW.OUTLANDENTERTAINMENT.COM

SUBSUME
WWW.SUBSUMELIFE.COM

SORGHUM & SPEAR VOLUME ONE: HARVEST OF THE ALL-MOTHER
First Printing. Published by Outland Entertainment LLC, 3119 Gillham Road, Kansas City MO, 64109.

For international rights, please contact: jeremy@outlandentertainment.com.

Printed and bound in China

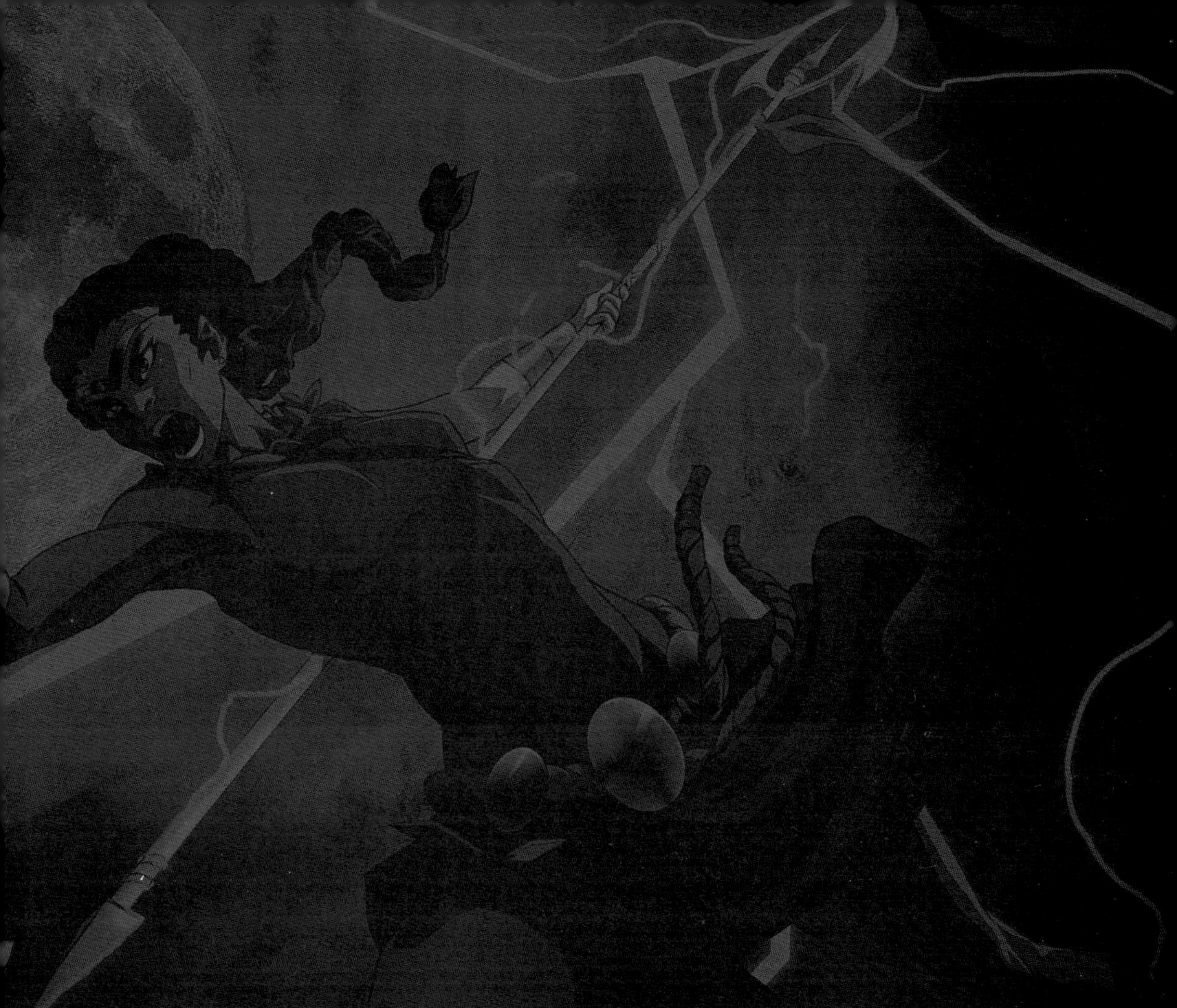

SORGHUM & SPEAR CREATED BY DEDREN SNEAD

WRITTEN BY DEDREN **SNEAD**

ILLUSTRATED BY WELINTHON **NOMMO**

LETTERS BY SAIDA **TEMOFONTE**

EDITED BY SARAH A. **MACKLIN**

EDITORIAL ASSISTS BY ROBERT **JEFFREY II**

EXECUTIVE PRODUCED BY NICHELLE **NICHOLS** AND **RAPSODY**

COVER DESIGN BY DANIEL **COTES**

BOOK DESIGN BY JEREMY D. **MOHLER**

VARIANT COVER BY BRIAN **STELFREEZE**

SPECIAL THANKS TO OUR KICKSTARTER BACKERS FOR THEIR LOVE, PATIENCE, AND SUPPORT.

WWW.SORGHUMANDSPEAR.COM

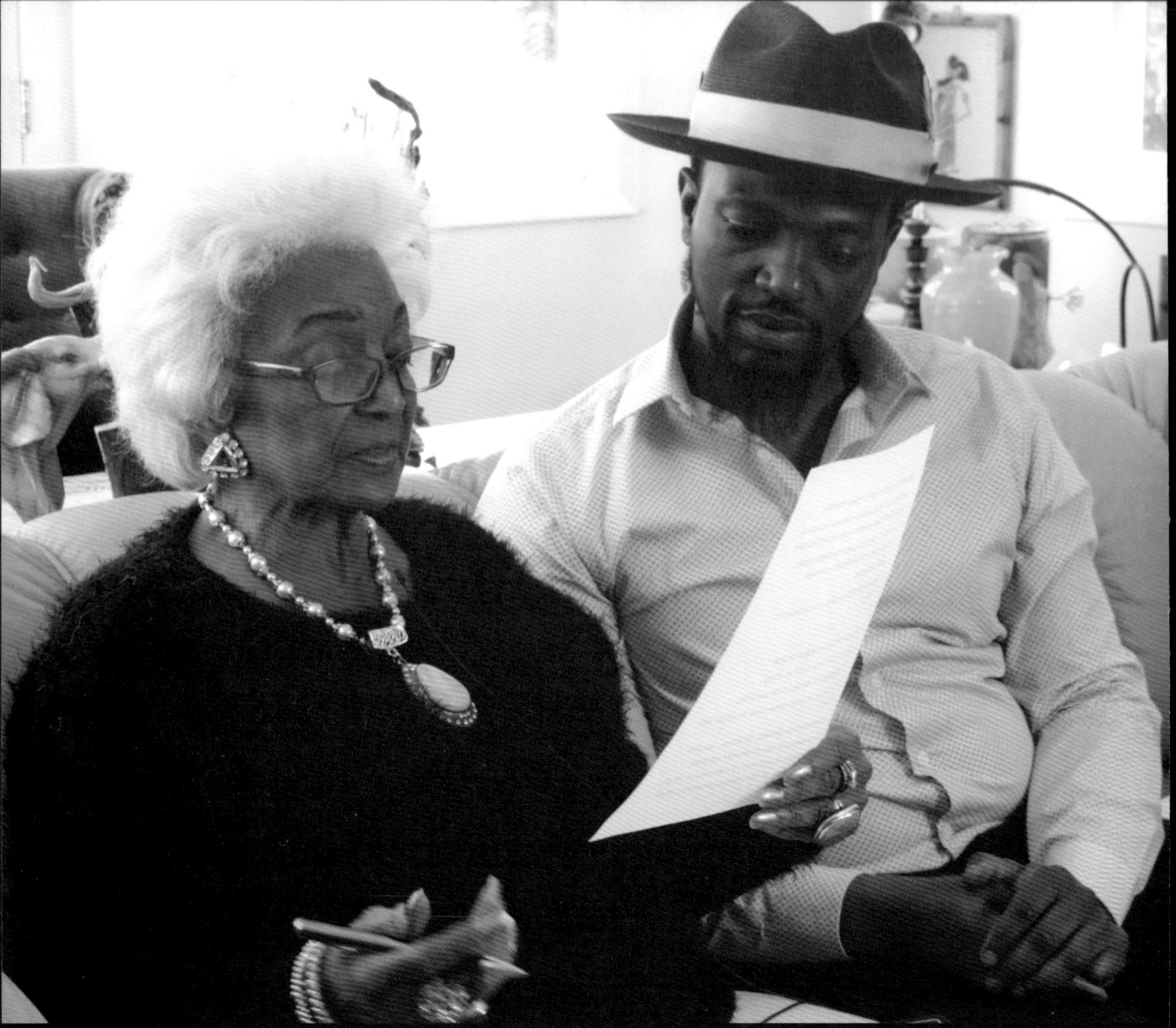

I still remember the very first time I saw her. She stole my heart, and I never asked for it back.

I was a young country boy in Snow Hill, North Carolina, spending one summer break afternoon parked in front of my uncle's new color television. He was the first person we knew that had gotten a new-fangled device installed in his backyard: a satellite dish.

I was sunk deep into a shaggy carpet strewn with toys and comic books, awaiting reception of the next transmission from space, when a new cartoon faded into view.

Star Trek: The Animated Series on Nickelodeon.

Immediately one character captivated my attention. She was intelligence, grace, talent, and beauty.

And she was Black like me.

From that moment on, I was enthralled by Lieutenant Nyota Uhura, and eventually her real-life performer, Nichelle Nichols.

Her representation and presence kindled a spark of creativity to build a world of women like her, where in so many other places I had looked and found nothing comparable.

And so, I decided to create something myself.

SORGHUM & SPEAR was first written during my college years as a role-playing module to satisfy a yearning to bring together my interest in Pan-Africanism with my passions for gaming and fantasy writing specifically through Dungeons & Dragons. I used those stories and characters to create my first independent comic, whose words and imagery found their way into her hands, and eventually into her heart.

Being able to craft your first project with your heroine is both a surreal and weighted experience.

A snapshot of a day at her home, working together:

We were writing a script and recording her character opening for our animated series' introduction.

To have her effortlessly lend her elegance, power, and beauty to her character, ESHE THE ALL-MOTHER, and give so much of her persona time was a dream come true. I would begin to call her "My Goddess" as we talked that day and in conversations forward, as she would grace me with an earned blush and smile in acknowledgement. Time seemed so hastened in her presence.

Legacy. That is the word we used as we spoke about it. This is a legacy. I pray that this book, and our efforts to come, will somehow capture the eternal gratitude and honor I hold for you.

This shared legacy you have blessed me with, I will always endeavor to make a blessing to others.

You created our world and you created me. Neither would exist without you.

For You My Goddess
Dedren Snead - SORGHUM & SPEAR

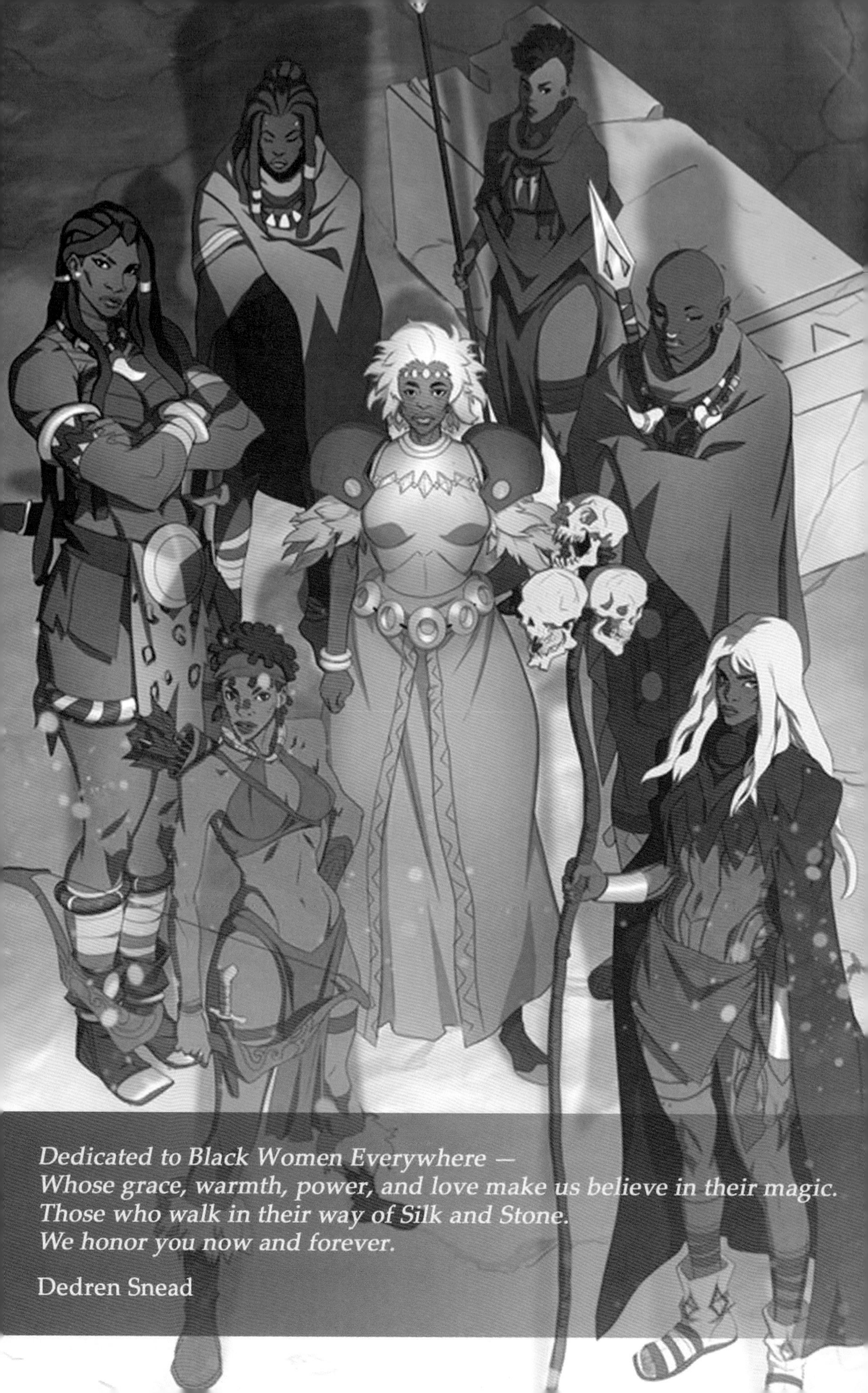

Dedicated to Black Women Everywhere —
Whose grace, warmth, power, and love make us believe in their magic.
Those who walk in their way of Silk and Stone.
We honor you now and forever.

Dedren Snead

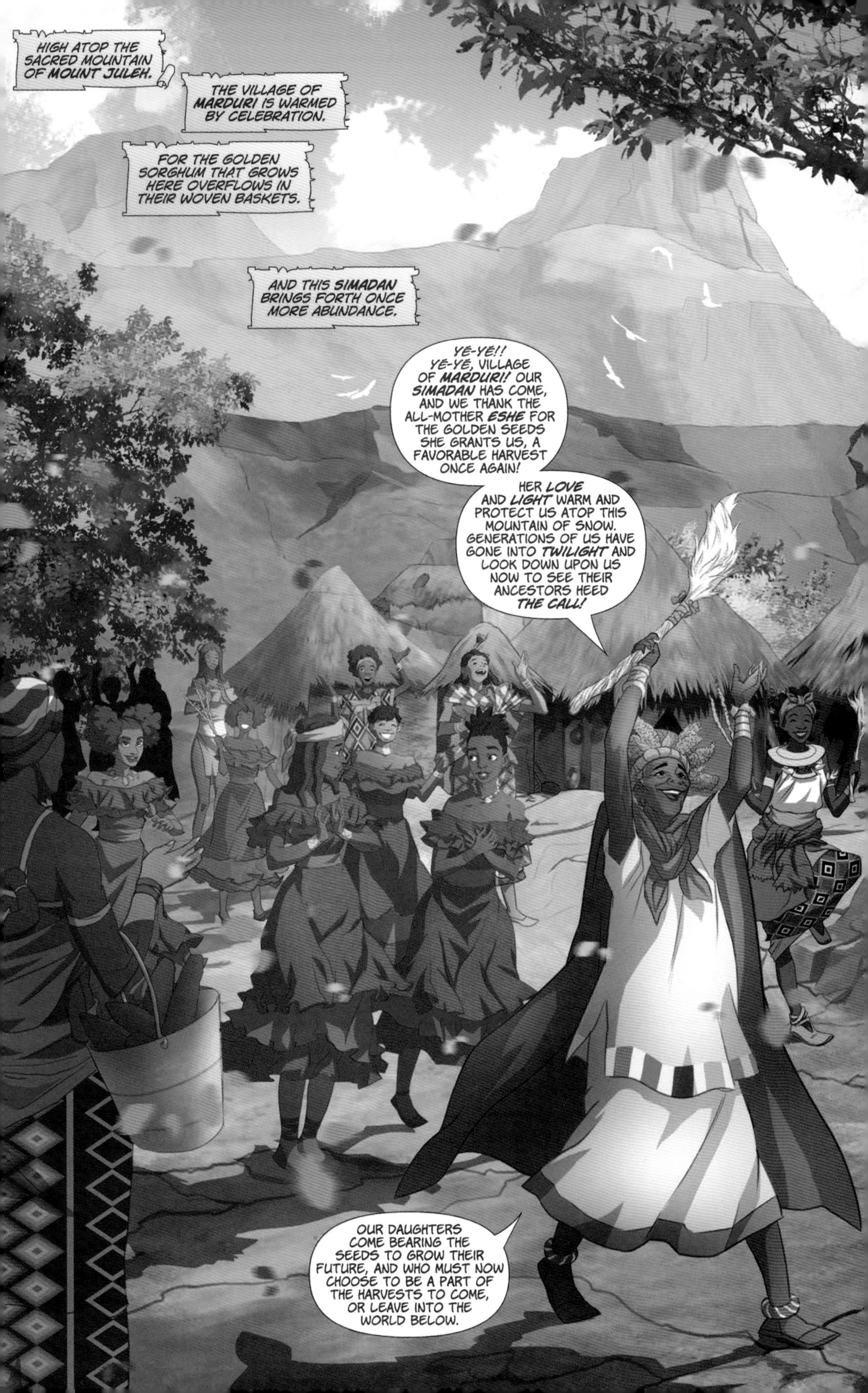
HIGH ATOP THE SACRED MOUNTAIN OF MOUNT JULEH.
THE VILLAGE OF MARDURI IS WARMED BY CELEBRATION.
FOR THE GOLDEN SORGHUM THAT GROWS HERE OVERFLOWS IN THEIR WOVEN BASKETS.
AND THIS SIMADAN BRINGS FORTH ONCE MORE ABUNDANCE.
YE-YE!! YE-YE, VILLAGE OF MARDURI!! OUR SIMADAN HAS COME, AND WE THANK THE ALL-MOTHER ESHE FOR THE GOLDEN SEEDS SHE GRANTS US, A FAVORABLE HARVEST ONCE AGAIN!
HER LOVE AND LIGHT WARM AND PROTECT US ATOP THIS MOUNTAIN OF SNOW. GENERATIONS OF US HAVE GONE INTO TWILIGHT AND LOOK DOWN UPON US NOW TO SEE THEIR ANCESTORS HEED THE CALL!
OUR DAUGHTERS COME BEARING THE SEEDS TO GROW THEIR FUTURE, AND WHO MUST NOW CHOOSE TO BE A PART OF THE HARVESTS TO COME, OR LEAVE INTO THE WORLD BELOW.

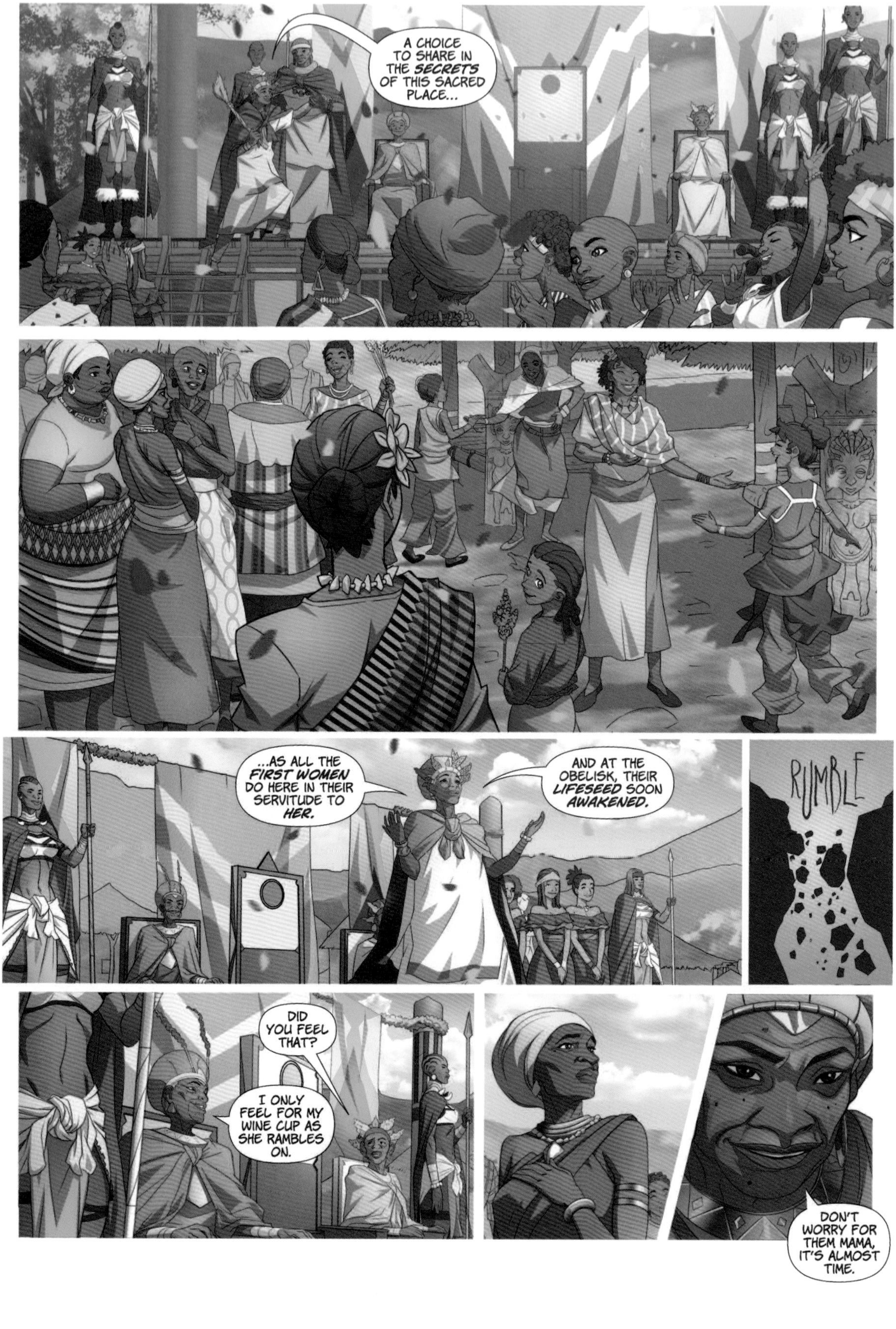
A CHOICE TO SHARE IN THE SECRETS OF THIS SACRED PLACE...
...AS ALL THE FIRST WOMEN DO HERE IN THEIR SERVITUDE TO HER.
AND AT THE OBELISK, THEIR LIFESEED SOON AWAKENED.
RUMBLE
DID YOU FEEL THAT?
I ONLY FEEL FOR MY WINE CUP AS SHE RAMBLES ON.
DON'T WORRY FOR THEM MAMA, IT'S ALMOST TIME.

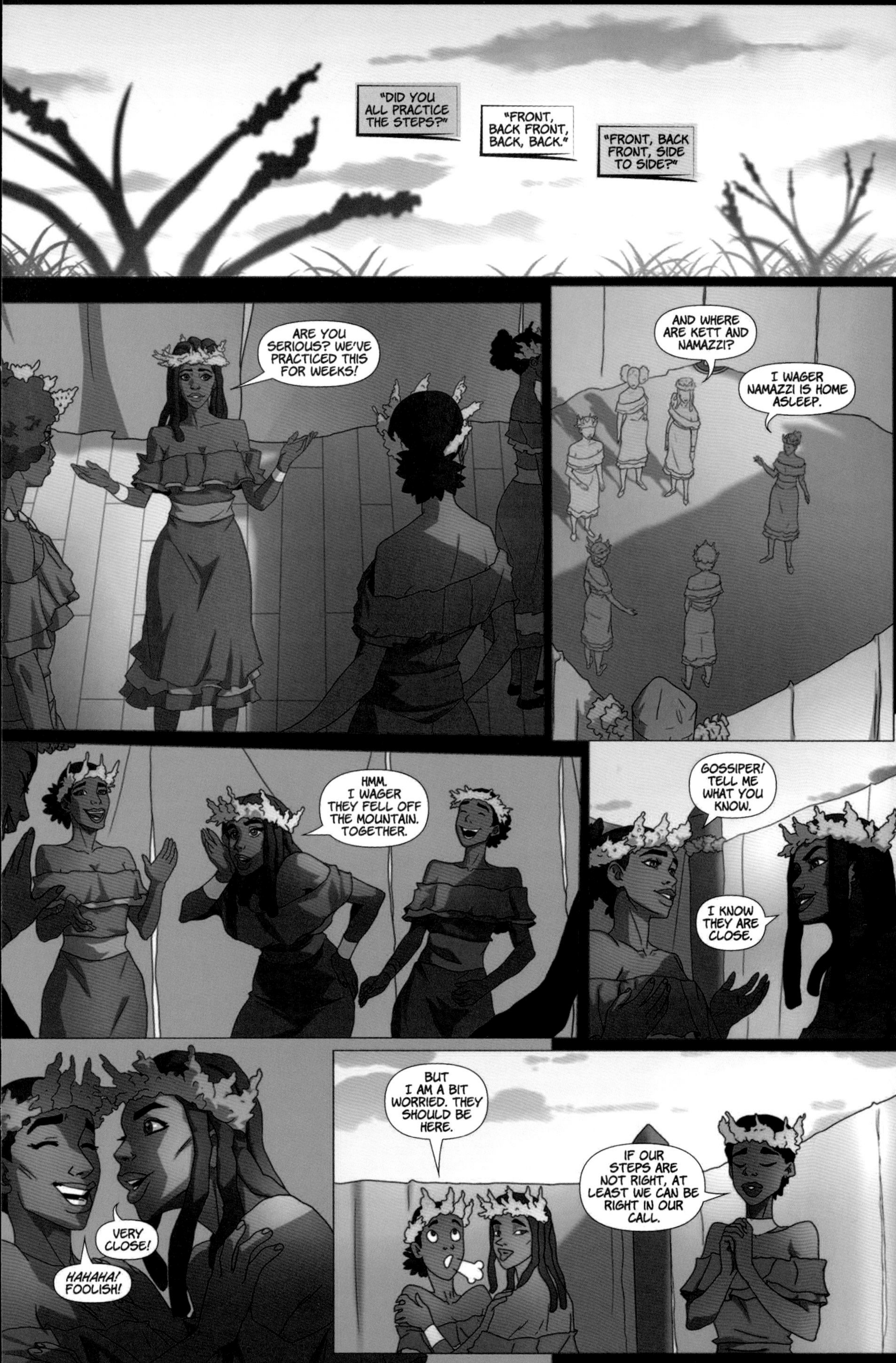

"DID YOU ALL PRACTICE THE STEPS?"
"FRONT, BACK FRONT, BACK, BACK."
"FRONT, BACK FRONT, SIDE TO SIDE?"
ARE YOU SERIOUS? WE'VE PRACTICED THIS FOR WEEKS!
AND WHERE ARE KETT AND NAMAZZI?
I WAGER NAMAZZI IS HOME ASLEEP.
HMM. I WAGER THEY FELL OFF THE MOUNTAIN. TOGETHER.
GOSSIPER! TELL ME WHAT YOU KNOW.
I KNOW THEY ARE CLOSE.
VERY CLOSE!
HAHAHA! FOOLISH!
BUT I AM A BIT WORRIED. THEY SHOULD BE HERE.
IF OUR STEPS ARE NOT RIGHT, AT LEAST WE CAN BE RIGHT IN OUR CALL.

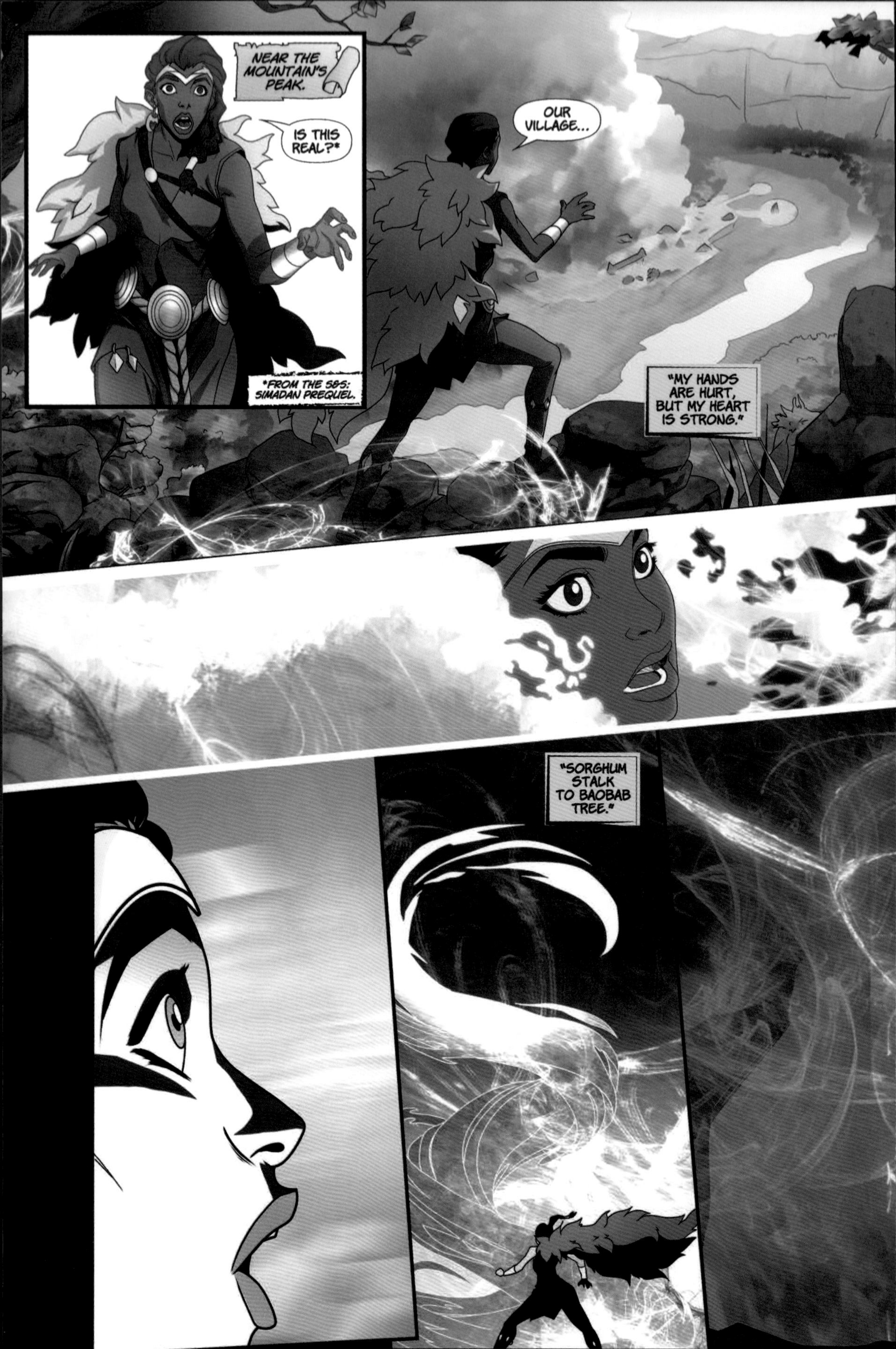
NEAR THE MOUNTAIN'S PEAK.
IS THIS REAL?*
*FROM THE S&S: SIMADAN PREQUEL.
OUR VILLAGE...
"MY HANDS ARE HURT, BUT MY HEART IS STRONG."
"SORGHUM STALK TO BAOBAB TREE."

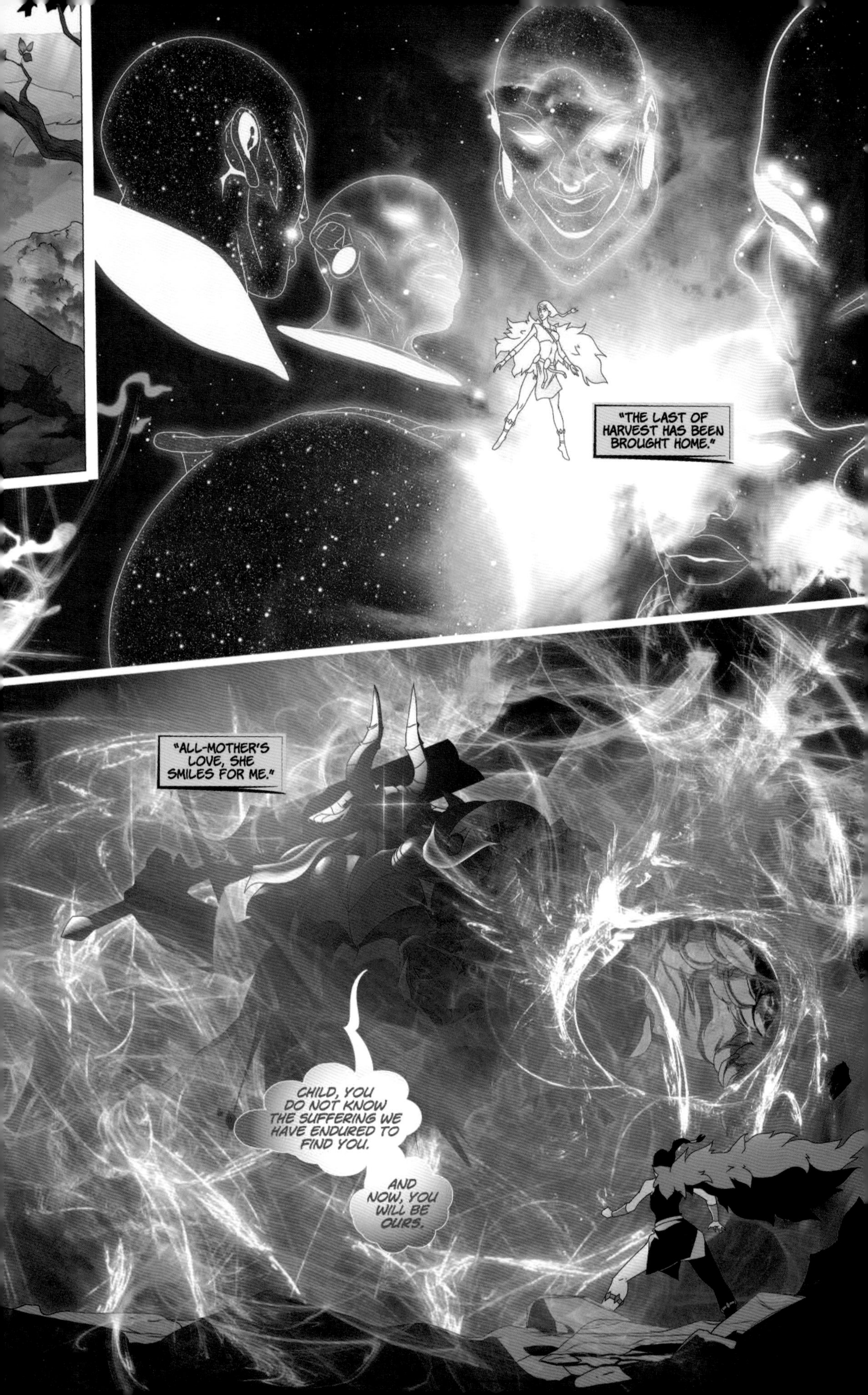
"THE LAST OF HARVEST HAS BEEN BROUGHT HOME."
"ALL-MOTHER'S LOVE, SHE SMILES FOR ME."
CHILD, YOU DO NOT KNOW THE SUFFERING WE HAVE ENDURED TO FIND YOU.
AND NOW, YOU WILL BE OURS.

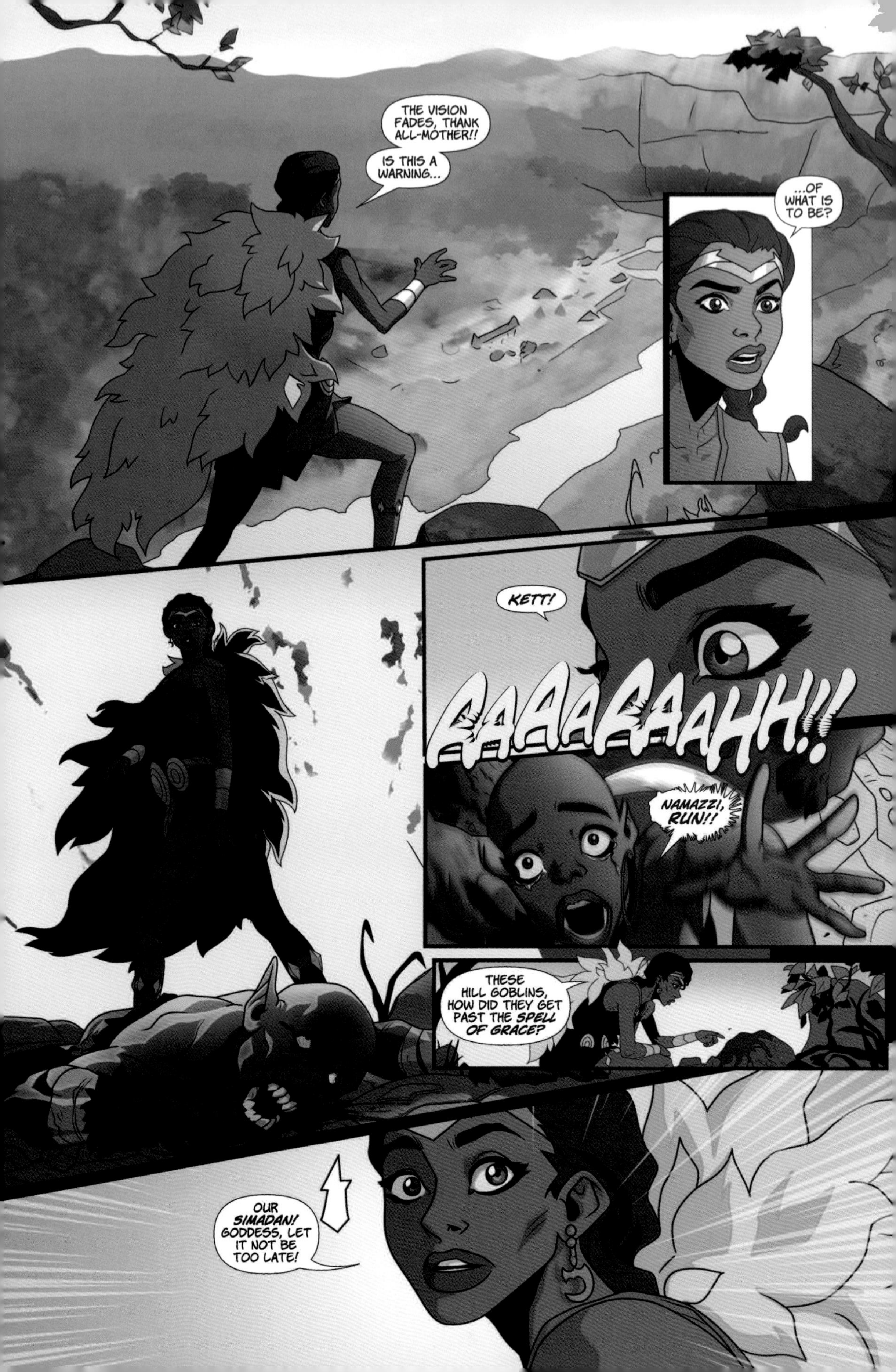
THE VISION FADES, THANK ALL-MOTHER!!
IS THIS A WARNING...
...OF WHAT IS TO BE?
KETT!
AAAARAAAHH!!
NAMAZZI, RUN!!
THESE HILL GOBLINS, HOW DID THEY GET PAST THE SPELL OF GRACE?
OUR SIMADAN! GODDESS, LET IT NOT BE TOO LATE!

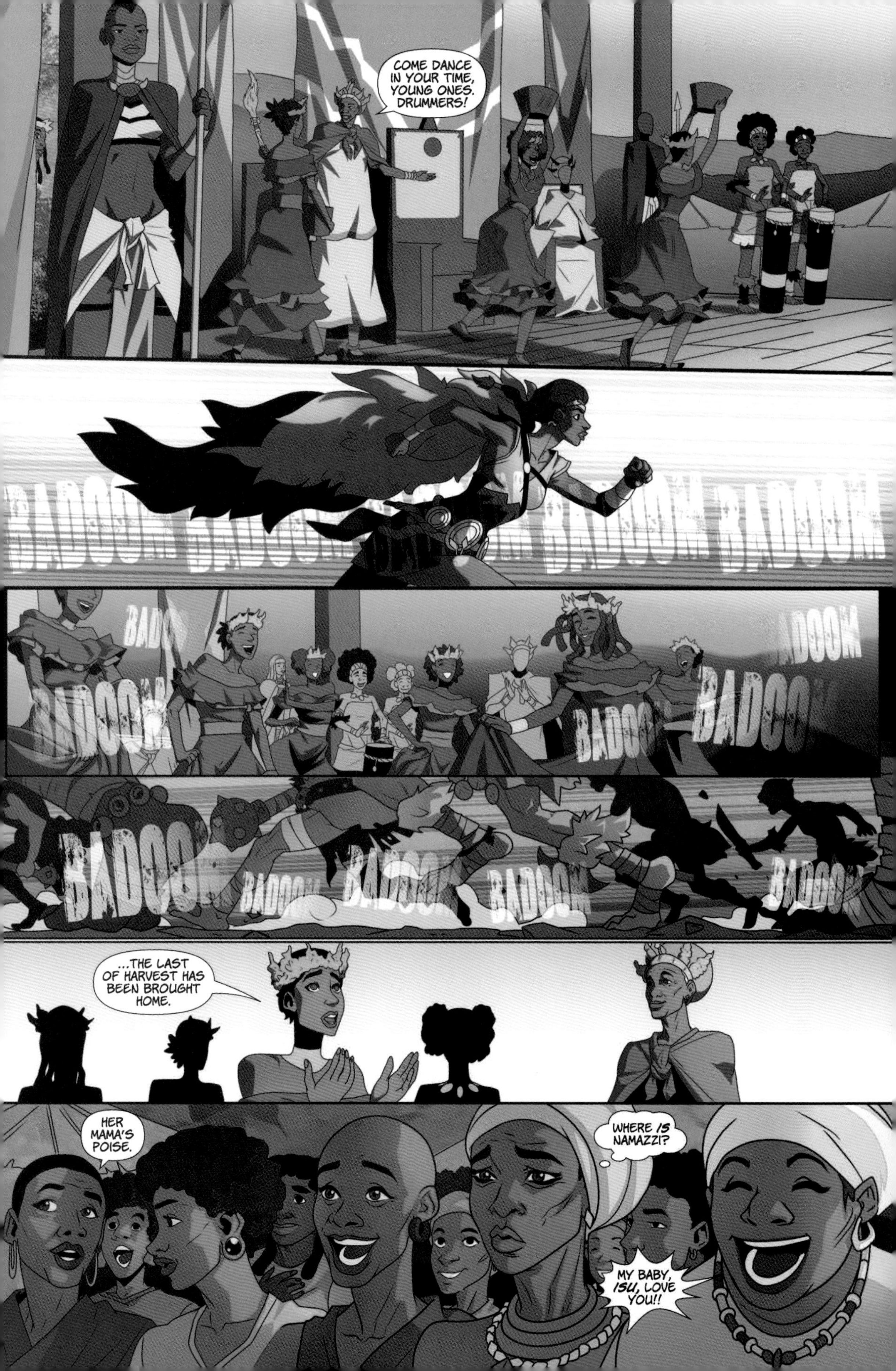
COME DANCE IN YOUR TIME, YOUNG ONES. DRUMMERS!
BADOOM BADOOM BADOOM BADOOM BADOOM
BADOOM
BADOOM
BADOOM
BADOOM
BADOO
BADOOM
BADOOM
BADOOM
BADOOM
BADOOM
...THE LAST OF HARVEST HAS BEEN BROUGHT HOME.
HER MAMA'S POISE.
WHERE *IS* NAMAZZI?
MY BABY, *ISU*, LOVE YOU!!

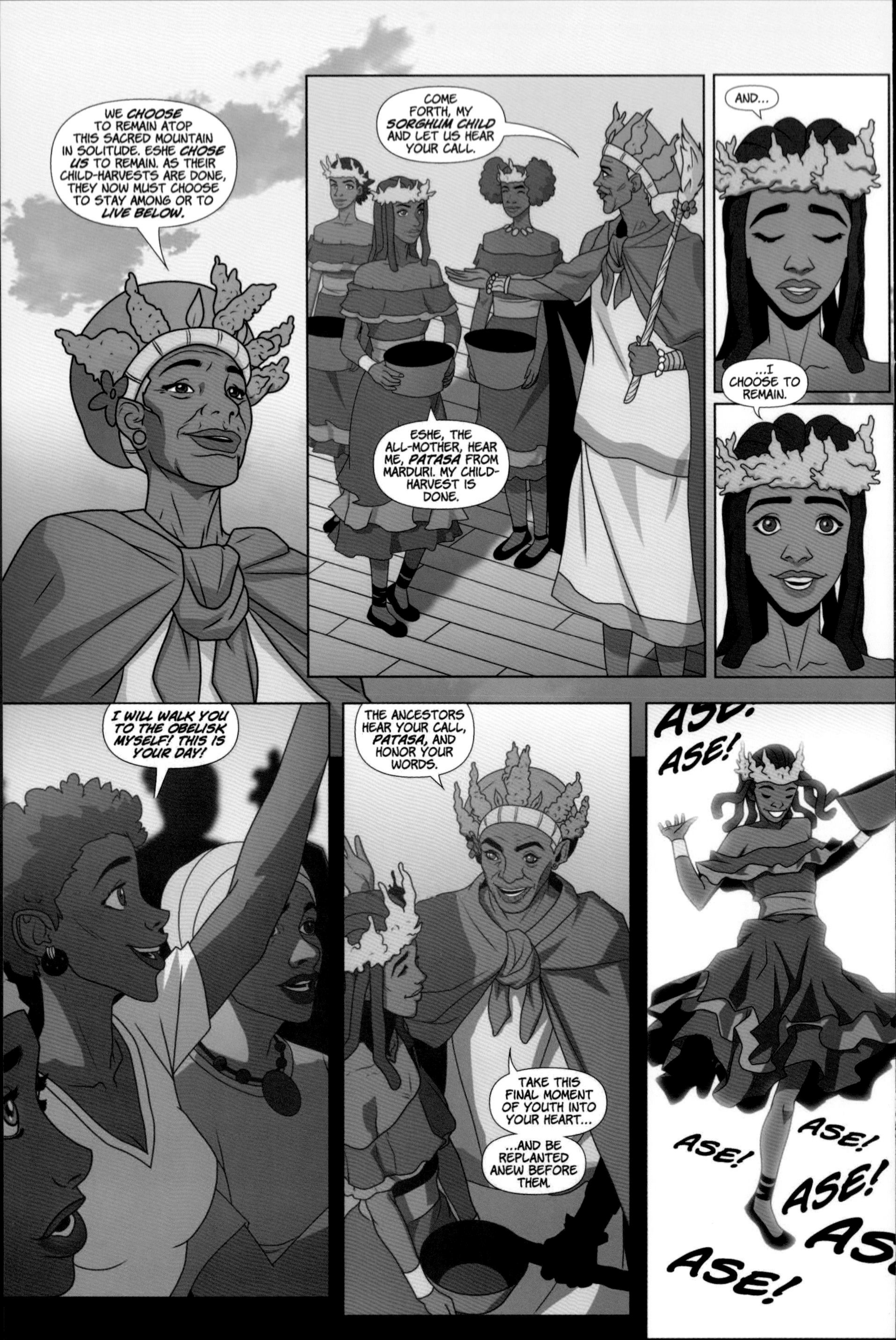

WE CHOOSE TO REMAIN ATOP THIS SACRED MOUNTAIN IN SOLITUDE. ESHE CHOSE US TO REMAIN. AS THEIR CHILD-HARVESTS ARE DONE, THEY NOW MUST CHOOSE TO STAY AMONG OR TO LIVE BELOW.
COME FORTH, MY SORGHUM CHILD AND LET US HEAR YOUR CALL.
ESHE, THE ALL-MOTHER, HEAR ME, PATASA FROM MARDURI. MY CHILD-HARVEST IS DONE.
AND...
...I CHOOSE TO REMAIN.
I WILL WALK YOU TO THE OBELISK MYSELF! THIS IS YOUR DAY!
THE ANCESTORS HEAR YOUR CALL, PATASA, AND HONOR YOUR WORDS.
TAKE THIS FINAL MOMENT OF YOUTH INTO YOUR HEART...
...AND BE REPLANTED ANEW BEFORE THEM.
ASE!
ASE!
ASE!
ASE!
ASE!

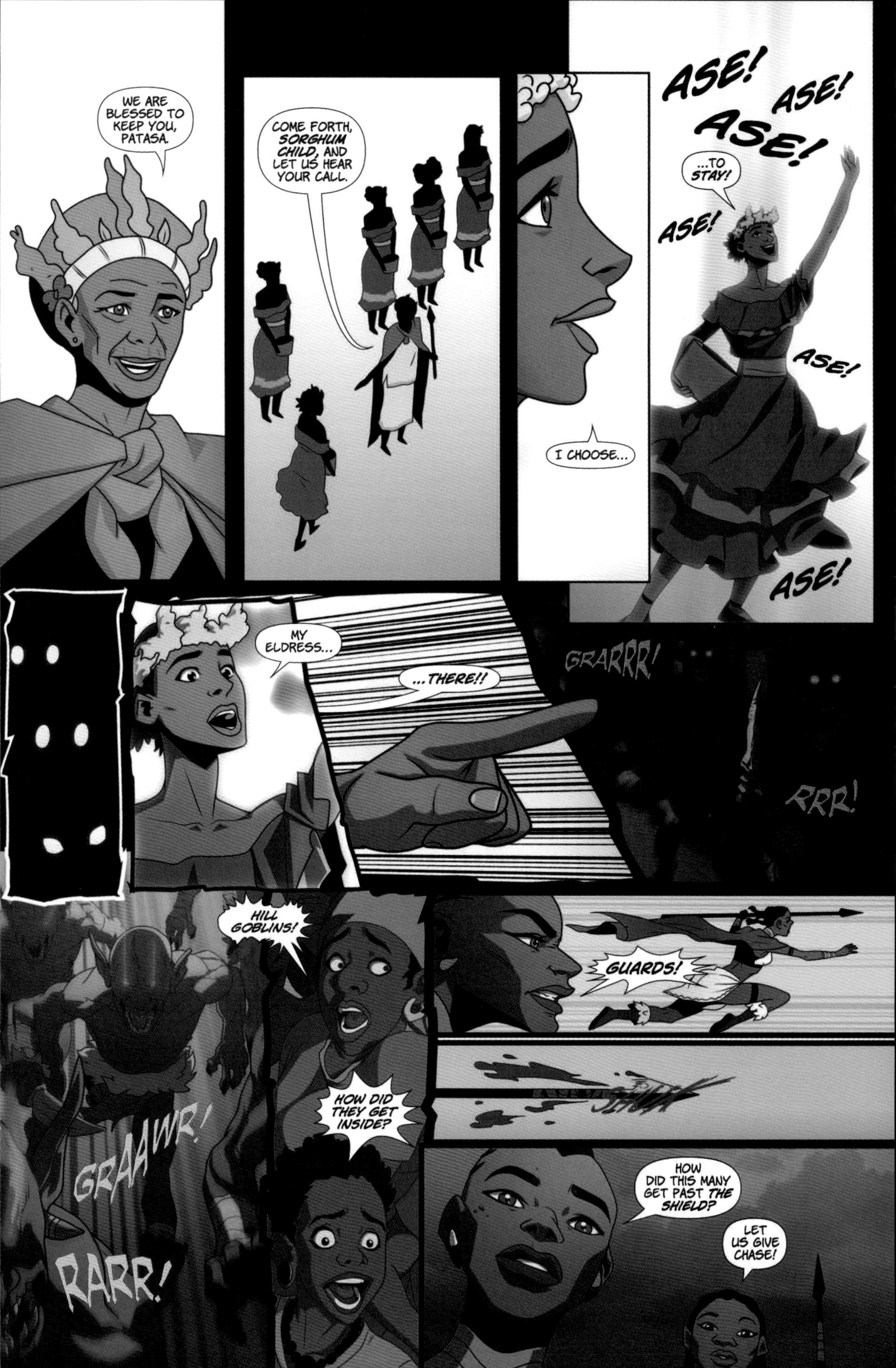
WE ARE BLESSED TO KEEP YOU, PATASA.
COME FORTH, SORGHUM CHILD, AND LET US HEAR YOUR CALL.
I CHOOSE...
ASE!
ASE!
ASE!
...TO STAY!
ASE!
ASE!
ASE!
MY ELDRESS...
...THERE!!
GRARRR!
RRR!
HILL GOBLINS!
GUARDS!
HOW DID THEY GET INSIDE?
GRAAWR!
RARR!
HOW DID THIS MANY GET PAST THE SHIELD?
LET US GIVE CHASE!

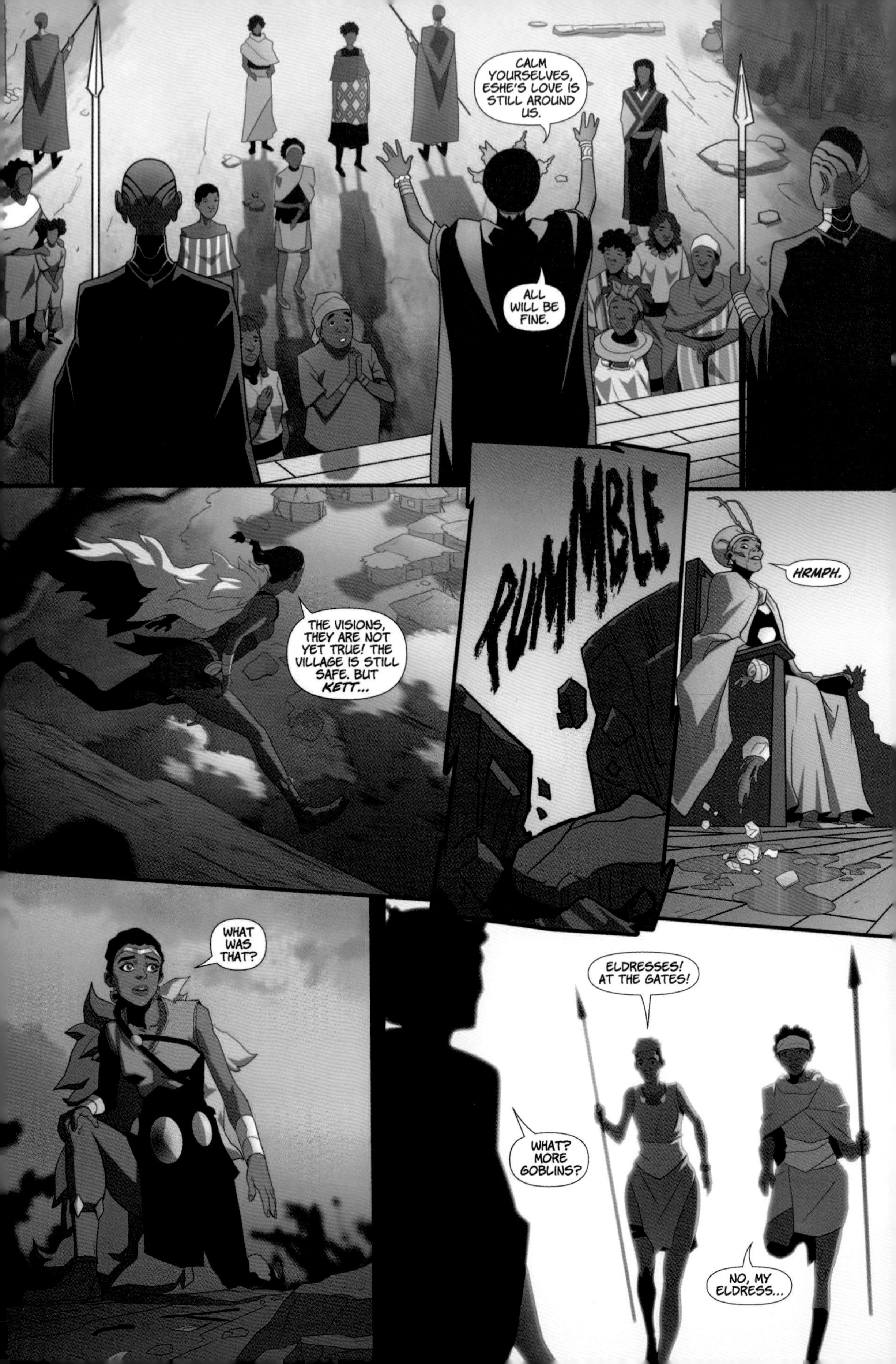
CALM YOURSELVES, ESHE'S LOVE IS STILL AROUND US.
ALL WILL BE FINE.
THE VISIONS, THEY ARE NOT YET TRUE! THE VILLAGE IS STILL SAFE. BUT KETT...
RUMMBLE
HRMPH.
WHAT WAS THAT?
ELDRESSES! AT THE GATES!
WHAT? MORE GOBLINS?
NO, MY ELDRESS...

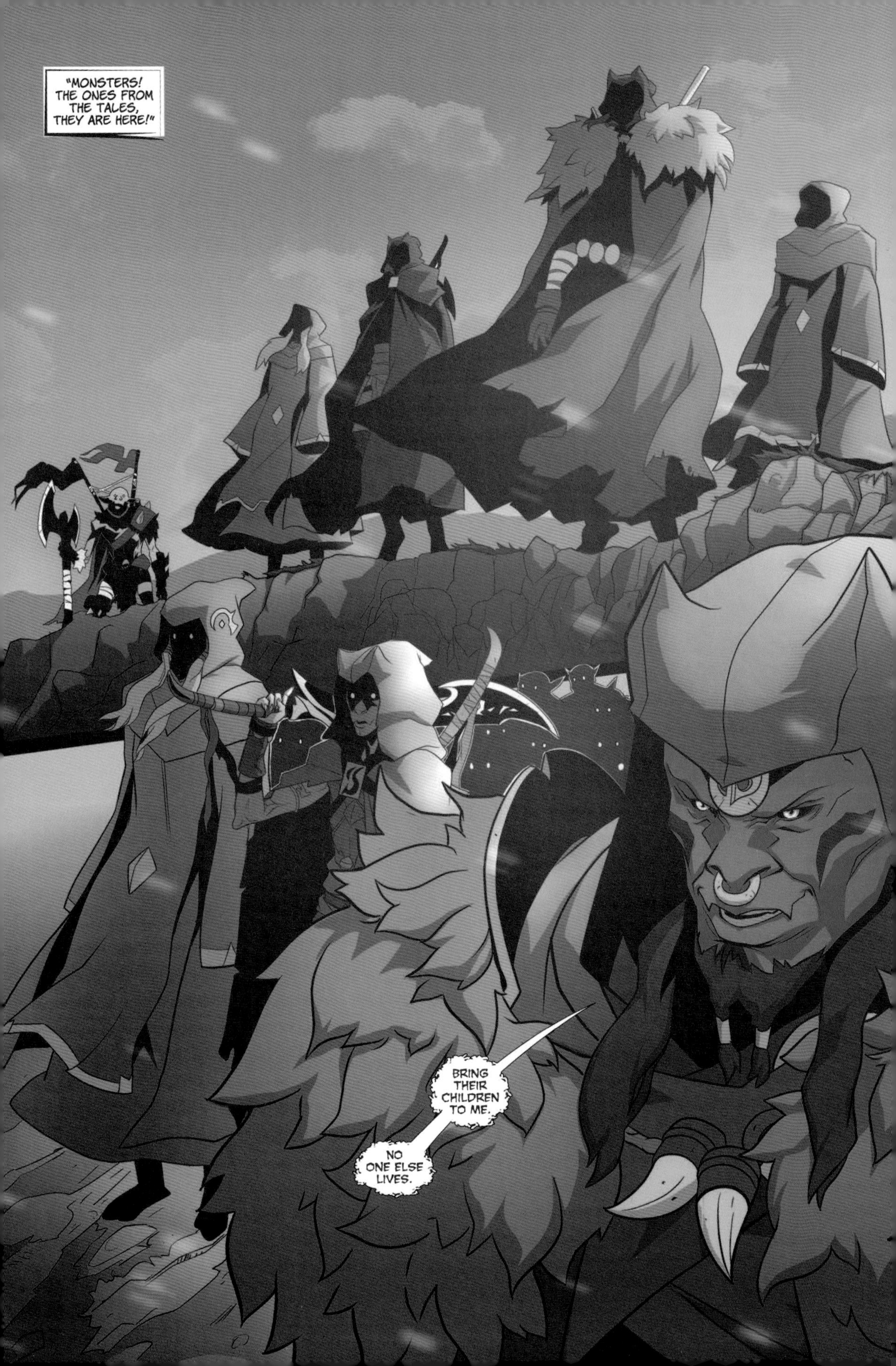
"MONSTERS! THE ONES FROM THE TALES, THEY ARE HERE!"
BRING THEIR CHILDREN TO ME.
NO ONE ELSE LIVES.

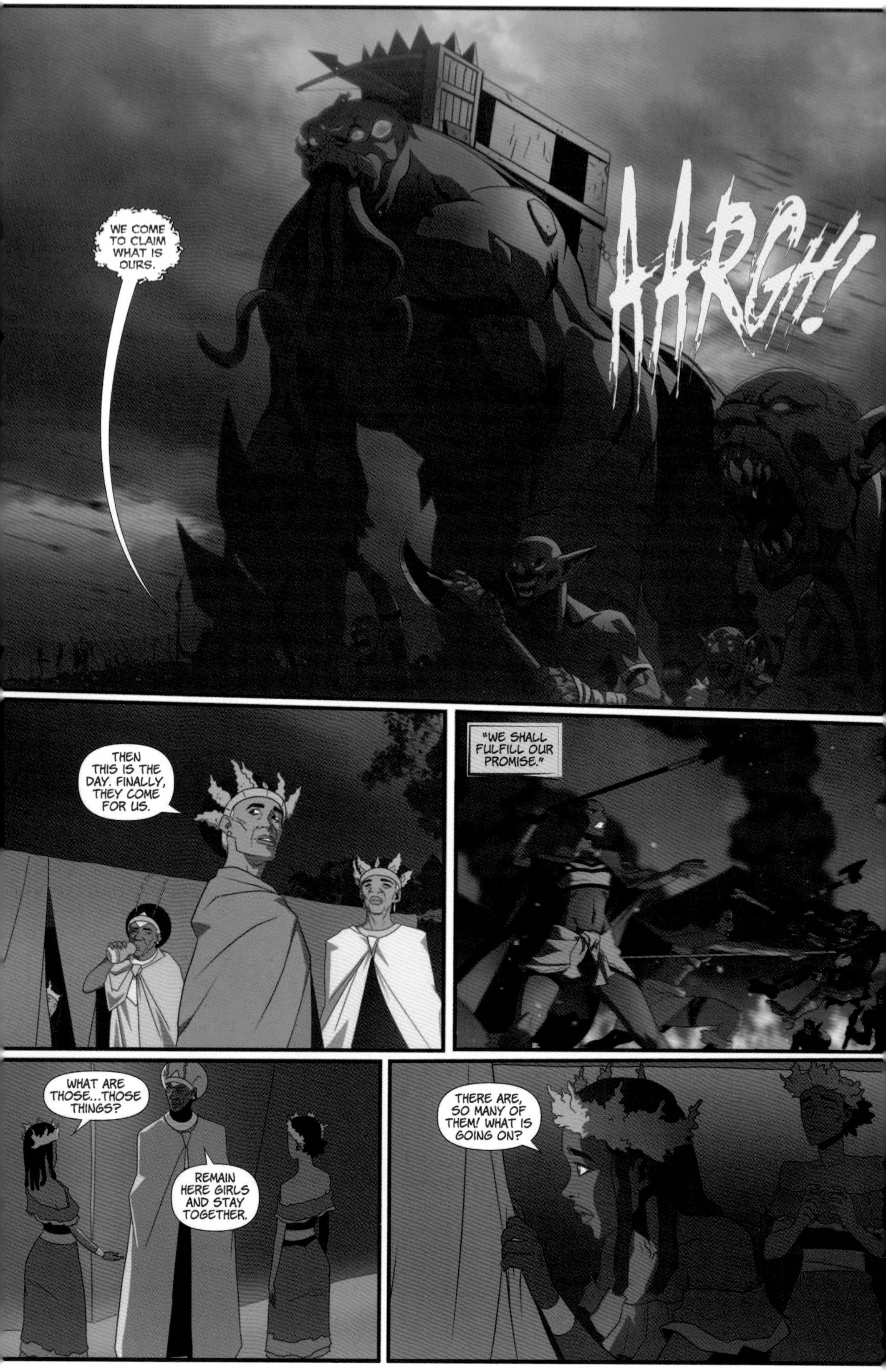

WE COME TO CLAIM WHAT IS OURS.
AARGH!
THEN THIS IS THE DAY. FINALLY, THEY COME FOR US.
"WE SHALL FULFILL OUR PROMISE."
WHAT ARE THOSE...THOSE THINGS?
REMAIN HERE GIRLS AND STAY TOGETHER.
THERE ARE, SO MANY OF THEM! WHAT IS GOING ON?

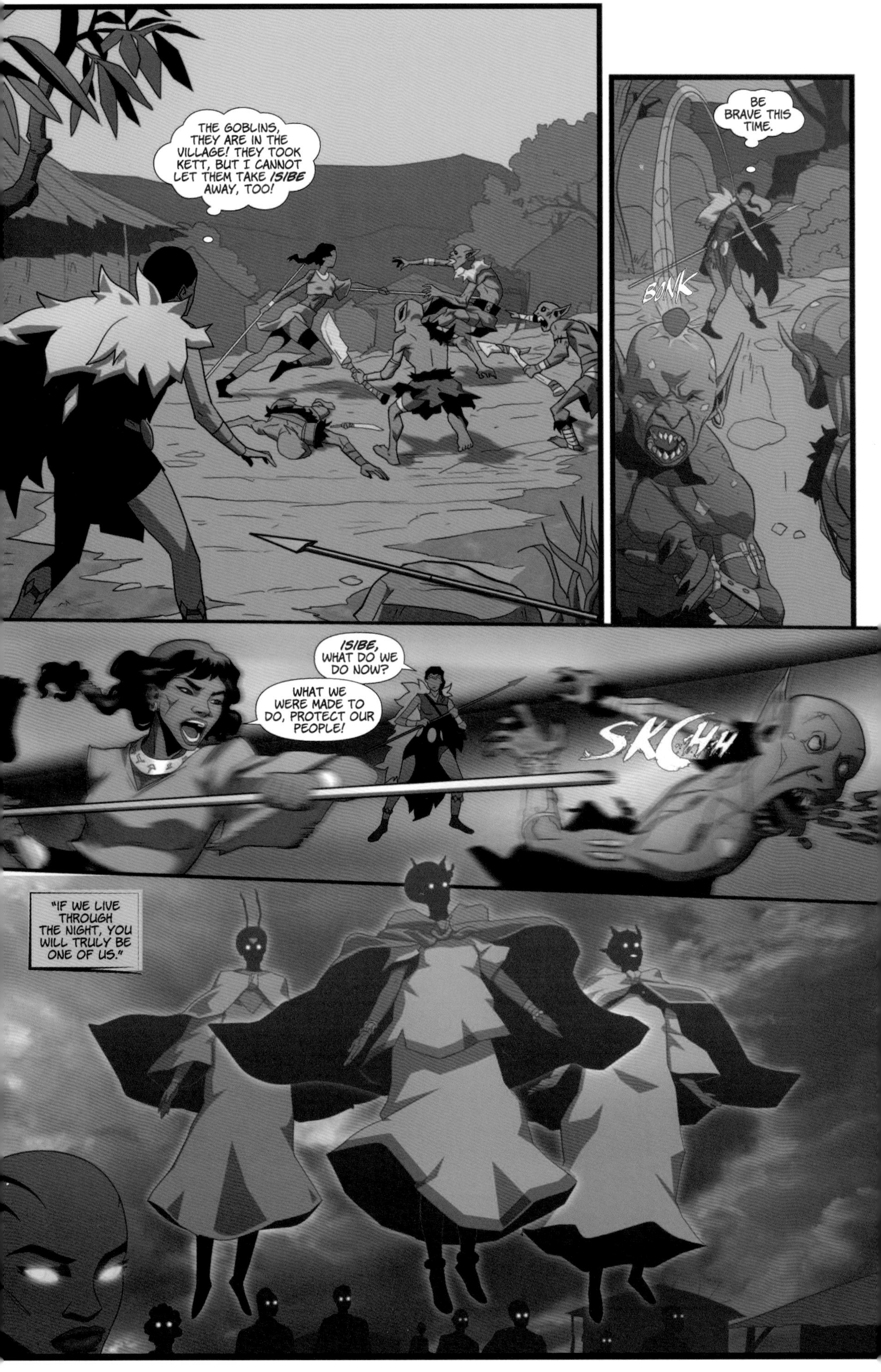
THE GOBLINS, THEY ARE IN THE VILLAGE! THEY TOOK KETT, BUT I CANNOT LET THEM TAKE *ISIBE* AWAY, TOO!
BE BRAVE THIS TIME.
BONK
ISIBE, WHAT DO WE DO NOW?
WHAT WE WERE MADE TO DO, PROTECT OUR PEOPLE!
SKCHH
"IF WE LIVE THROUGH THE NIGHT, YOU WILL TRULY BE ONE OF US."

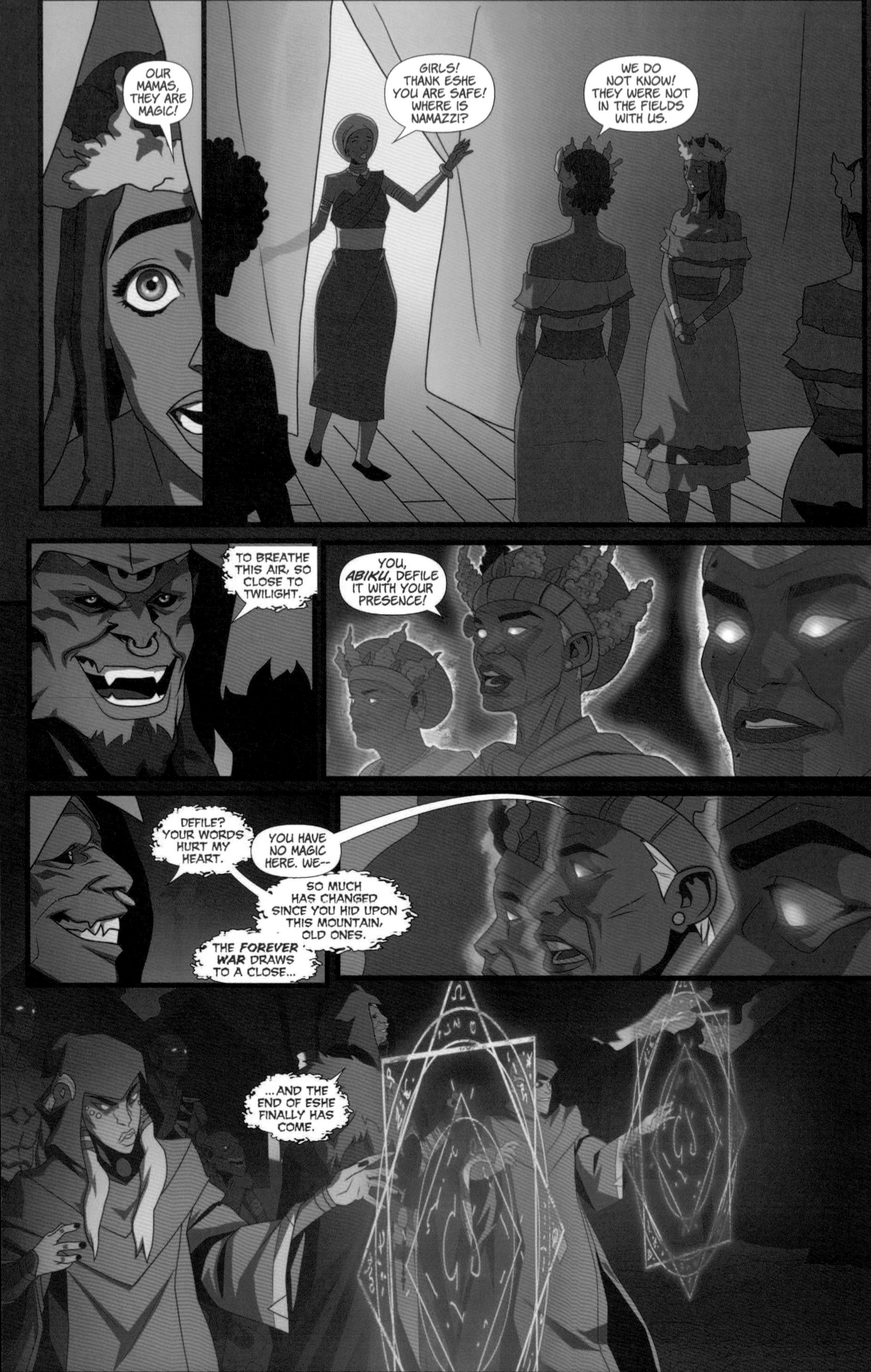
OUR MAMAS, THEY ARE MAGIC!
GIRLS! THANK ESHE YOU ARE SAFE! WHERE IS NAMAZZI?
WE DO NOT KNOW! THEY WERE NOT IN THE FIELDS WITH US.
TO BREATHE THIS AIR, SO CLOSE TO TWILIGHT.
YOU, ABIKU, DEFILE IT WITH YOUR PRESENCE!
DEFILE? YOUR WORDS HURT MY HEART.
YOU HAVE NO MAGIC HERE. WE--
SO MUCH HAS CHANGED SINCE YOU HID UPON THIS MOUNTAIN, OLD ONES.
THE FOREVER WAR DRAWS TO A CLOSE...
...AND THE END OF ESHE FINALLY HAS COME.

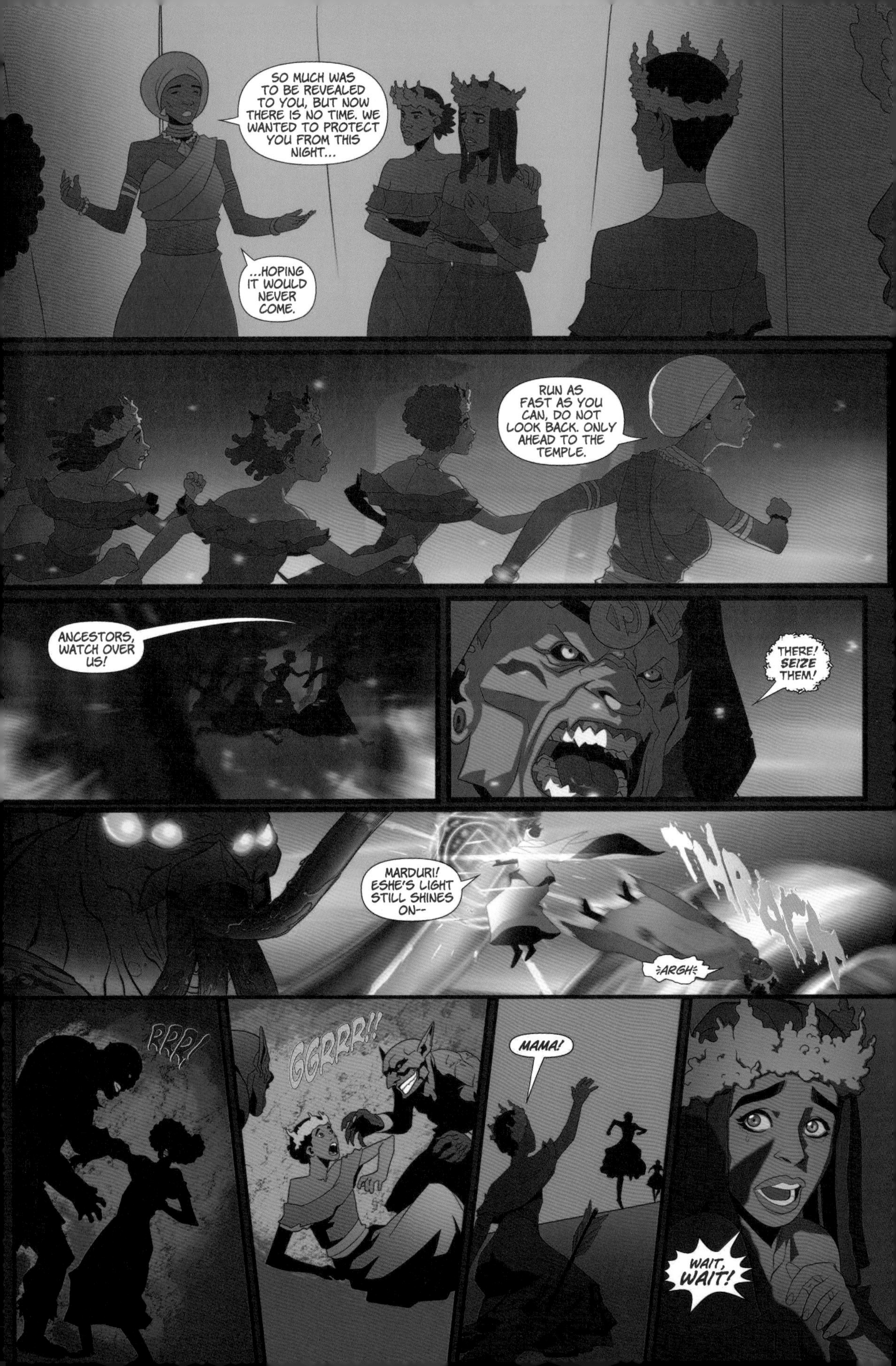
SO MUCH WAS TO BE REVEALED TO YOU, BUT NOW THERE IS NO TIME. WE WANTED TO PROTECT YOU FROM THIS NIGHT...
...HOPING IT WOULD NEVER COME.
RUN AS FAST AS YOU CAN, DO NOT LOOK BACK. ONLY AHEAD TO THE TEMPLE.
ANCESTORS, WATCH OVER US!
THERE! SEIZE THEM!
MARDURI! ESHE'S LIGHT STILL SHINES ON--
THRAAKK
ARGH
RRR!
GGRRR!!
MAMA!
WAIT, WAIT!

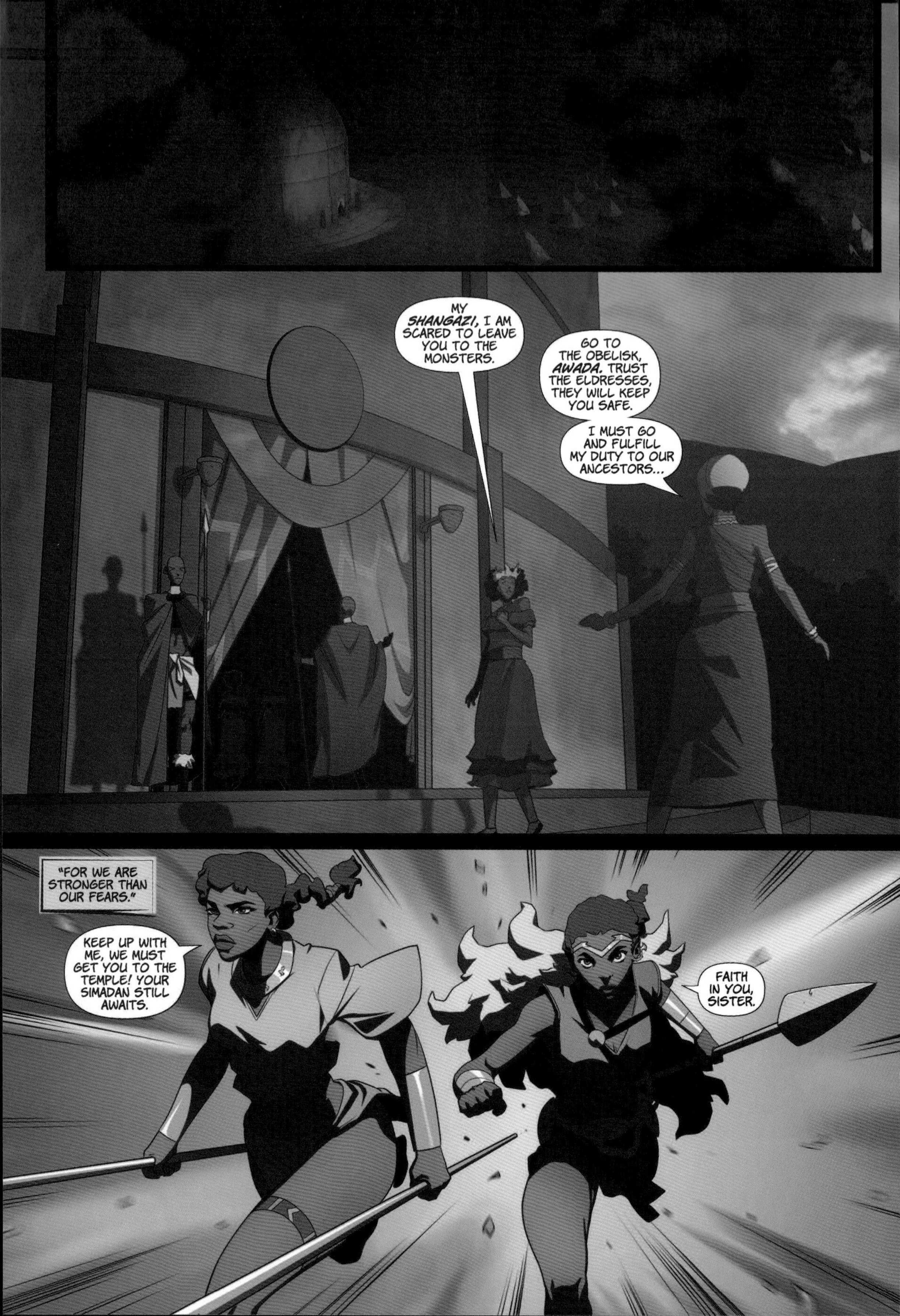
MY SHANGAZI, I AM SCARED TO LEAVE YOU TO THE MONSTERS.
GO TO THE OBELISK, AWADA. TRUST THE ELDRESSES, THEY WILL KEEP YOU SAFE.
I MUST GO AND FULFILL MY DUTY TO OUR ANCESTORS...
"FOR WE ARE STRONGER THAN OUR FEARS."
KEEP UP WITH ME, WE MUST GET YOU TO THE TEMPLE! YOUR SIMADAN STILL AWAITS.
FAITH IN YOU, SISTER.

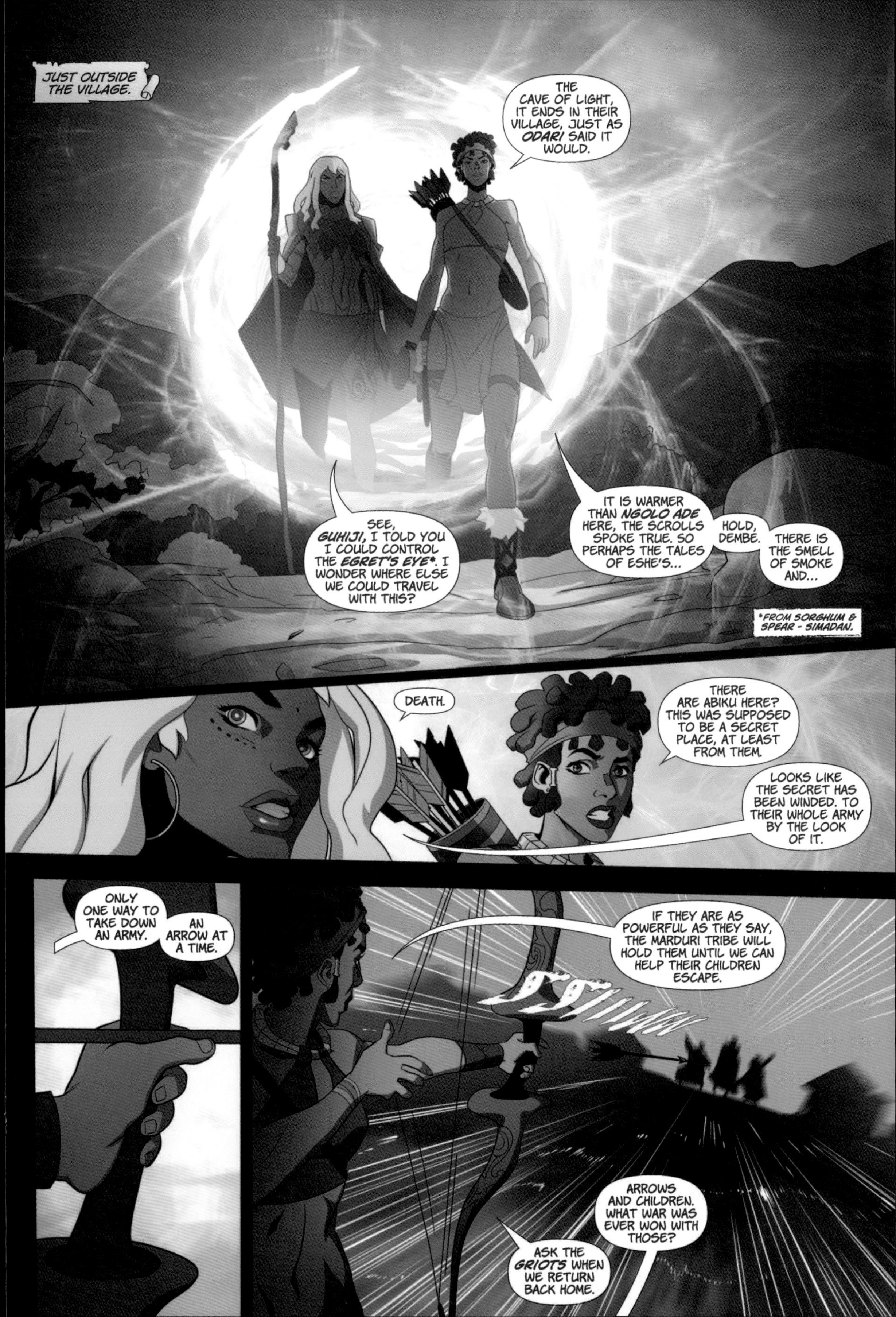

JUST OUTSIDE THE VILLAGE.
THE CAVE OF LIGHT, IT ENDS IN THEIR VILLAGE, JUST AS ODARI SAID IT WOULD.
SEE, GUHIJI, I TOLD YOU I COULD CONTROL THE EGRET'S EYE*. I WONDER WHERE ELSE WE COULD TRAVEL WITH THIS?
IT IS WARMER THAN NGOLO ADE HERE, THE SCROLLS SPOKE TRUE. SO PERHAPS THE TALES OF ESHE'S...
HOLD, DEMBE.
THERE IS THE SMELL OF SMOKE AND...
*FROM SORGHUM & SPEAR - SIMADAN.
DEATH.
THERE ARE ABIKU HERE? THIS WAS SUPPOSED TO BE A SECRET PLACE, AT LEAST FROM THEM.
LOOKS LIKE THE SECRET HAS BEEN WINDED. TO THEIR WHOLE ARMY BY THE LOOK OF IT.
ONLY ONE WAY TO TAKE DOWN AN ARMY.
AN ARROW AT A TIME.
IF THEY ARE AS POWERFUL AS THEY SAY, THE MARDURI TRIBE WILL HOLD THEM UNTIL WE CAN HELP THEIR CHILDREN ESCAPE.
SSSHWWW
ARROWS AND CHILDREN. WHAT WAR WAS EVER WON WITH THOSE?
ASK THE GRIOTS WHEN WE RETURN BACK HOME.

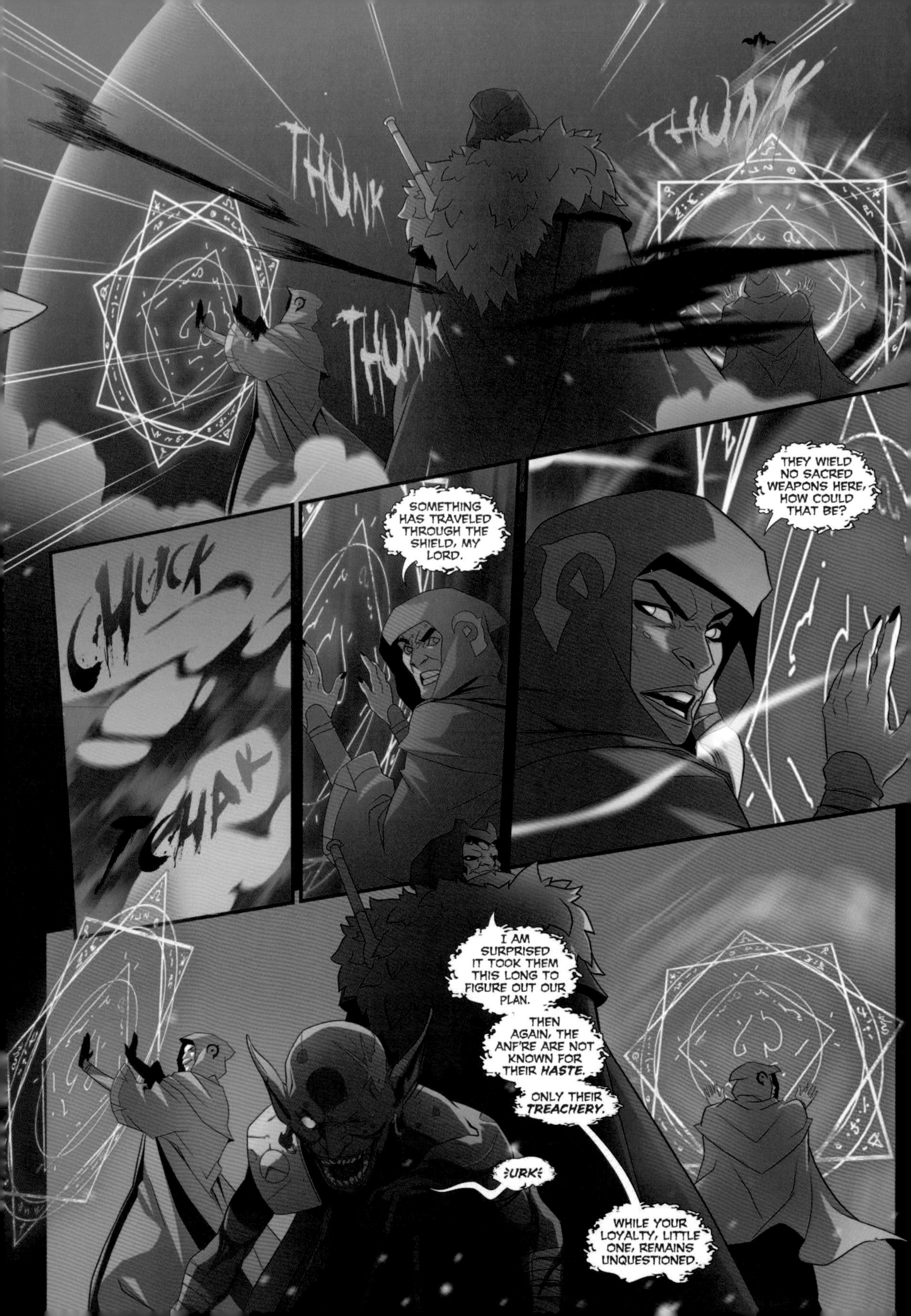
THUNK
THUNK
THUNK
CHUCK
TCHAK
SOMETHING HAS TRAVELED THROUGH THE SHIELD, MY LORD.
THEY WIELD NO SACRED WEAPONS HERE, HOW COULD THAT BE?
I AM SURPRISED IT TOOK THEM THIS LONG TO FIGURE OUT OUR PLAN.
THEN AGAIN, THE ANF'RE ARE NOT KNOWN FOR THEIR HASTE.
ONLY THEIR TREACHERY.
URK
WHILE YOUR LOYALTY, LITTLE ONE, REMAINS UNQUESTIONED.

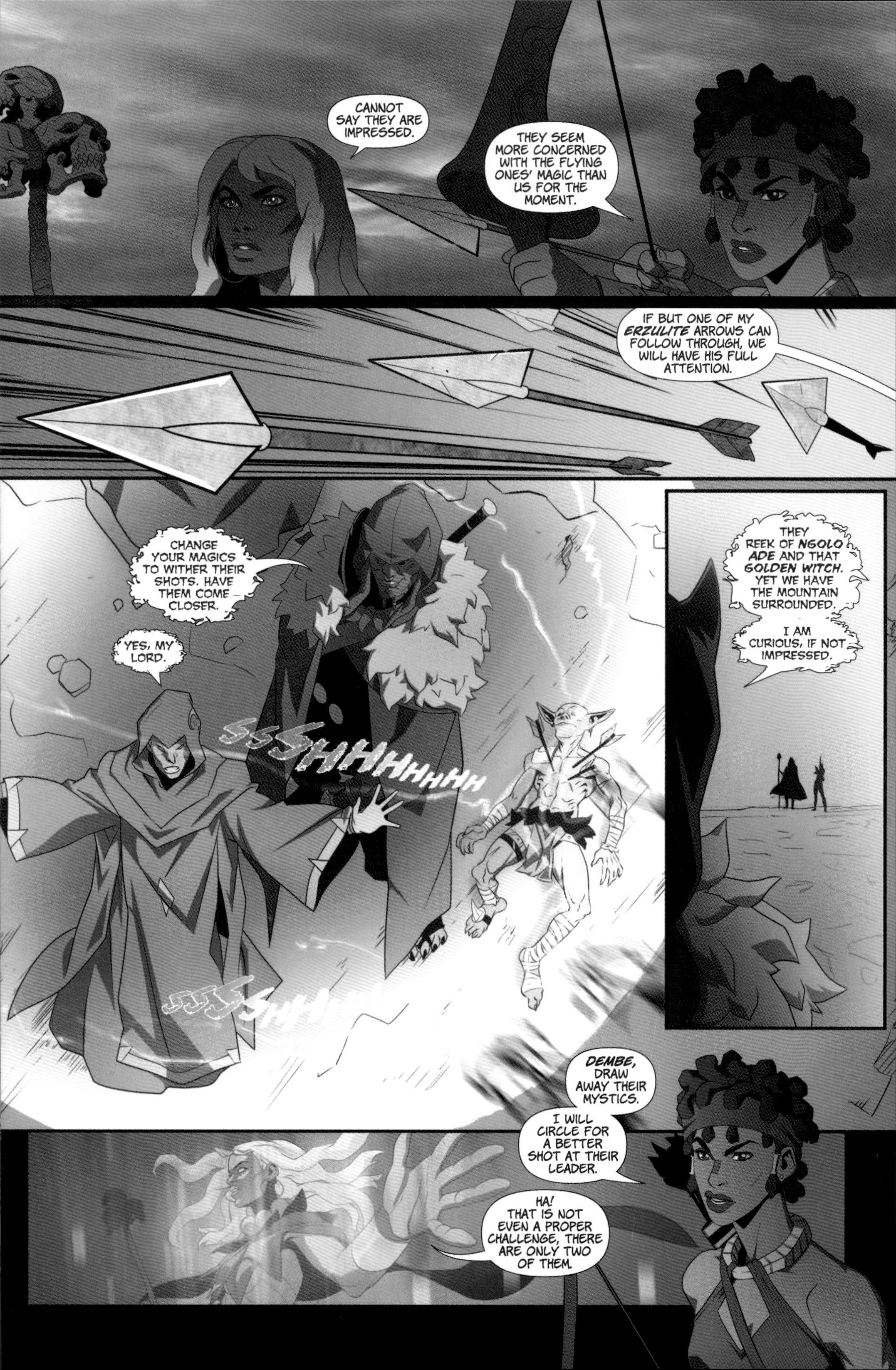

CANNOT SAY THEY ARE IMPRESSED.
THEY SEEM MORE CONCERNED WITH THE FLYING ONES' MAGIC THAN US FOR THE MOMENT.
IF BUT ONE OF MY ERZULITE ARROWS CAN FOLLOW THROUGH, WE WILL HAVE HIS FULL ATTENTION.
CHANGE YOUR MAGICS TO WITHER THEIR SHOTS. HAVE THEM COME CLOSER.
YES, MY LORD.
SSSHHHHHHHH
SSSSHHH
THEY REEK OF NGOLO ADE AND THAT GOLDEN WITCH. YET WE HAVE THE MOUNTAIN SURROUNDED.
I AM CURIOUS, IF NOT IMPRESSED.
DEMBE, DRAW AWAY THEIR MYSTICS.
I WILL CIRCLE FOR A BETTER SHOT AT THEIR LEADER.
HA! THAT IS NOT EVEN A PROPER CHALLENGE, THERE ARE ONLY TWO OF THEM.

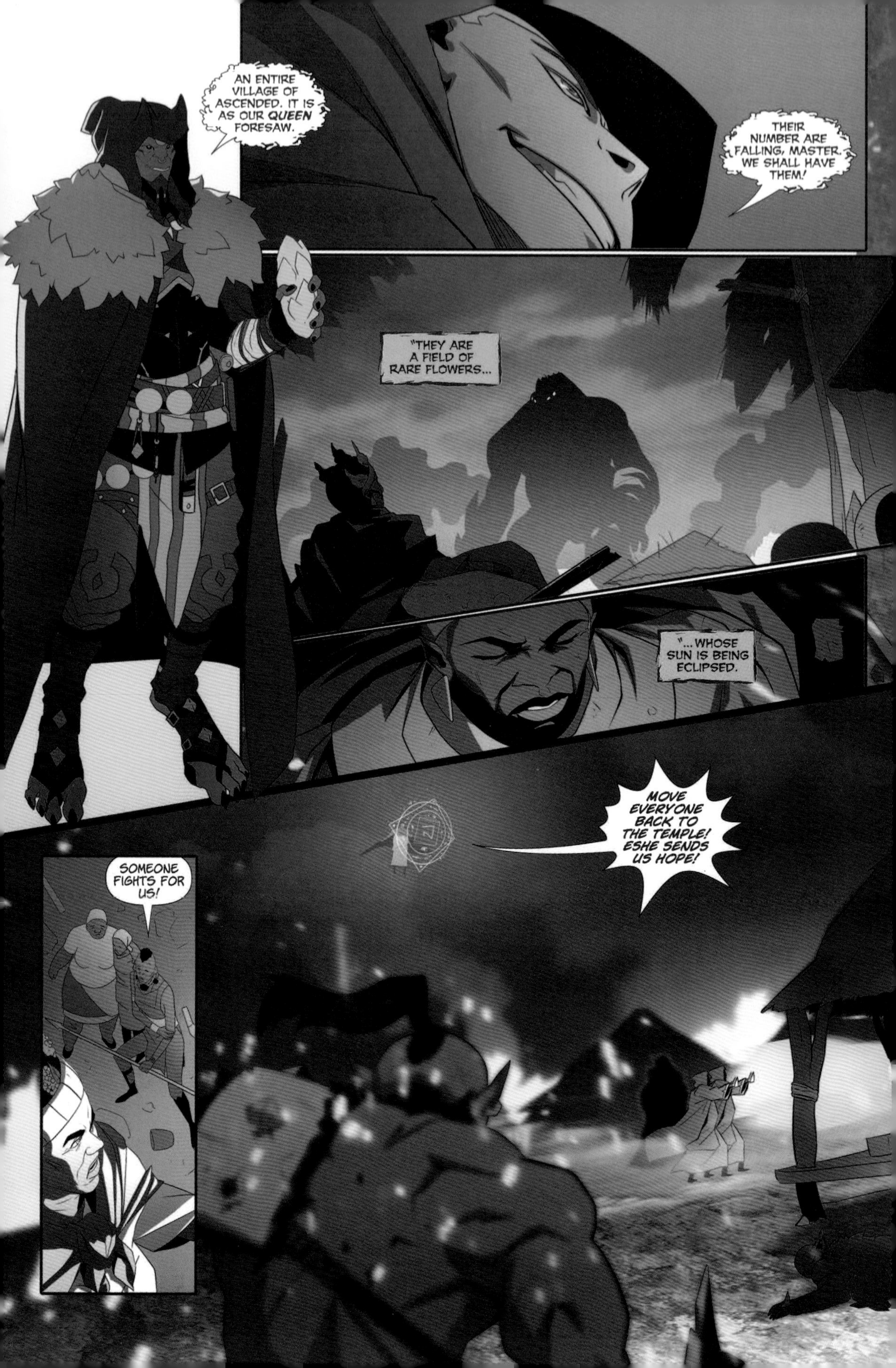
AN ENTIRE VILLAGE OF ASCENDED. IT IS AS OUR QUEEN FORESAW.
THEIR NUMBER ARE FALLING, MASTER. WE SHALL HAVE THEM!
"THEY ARE A FIELD OF RARE FLOWERS...
"...WHOSE SUN IS BEING ECLIPSED.
MOVE EVERYONE BACK TO THE TEMPLE! ESHE SENDS US HOPE!
SOMEONE FIGHTS FOR US!

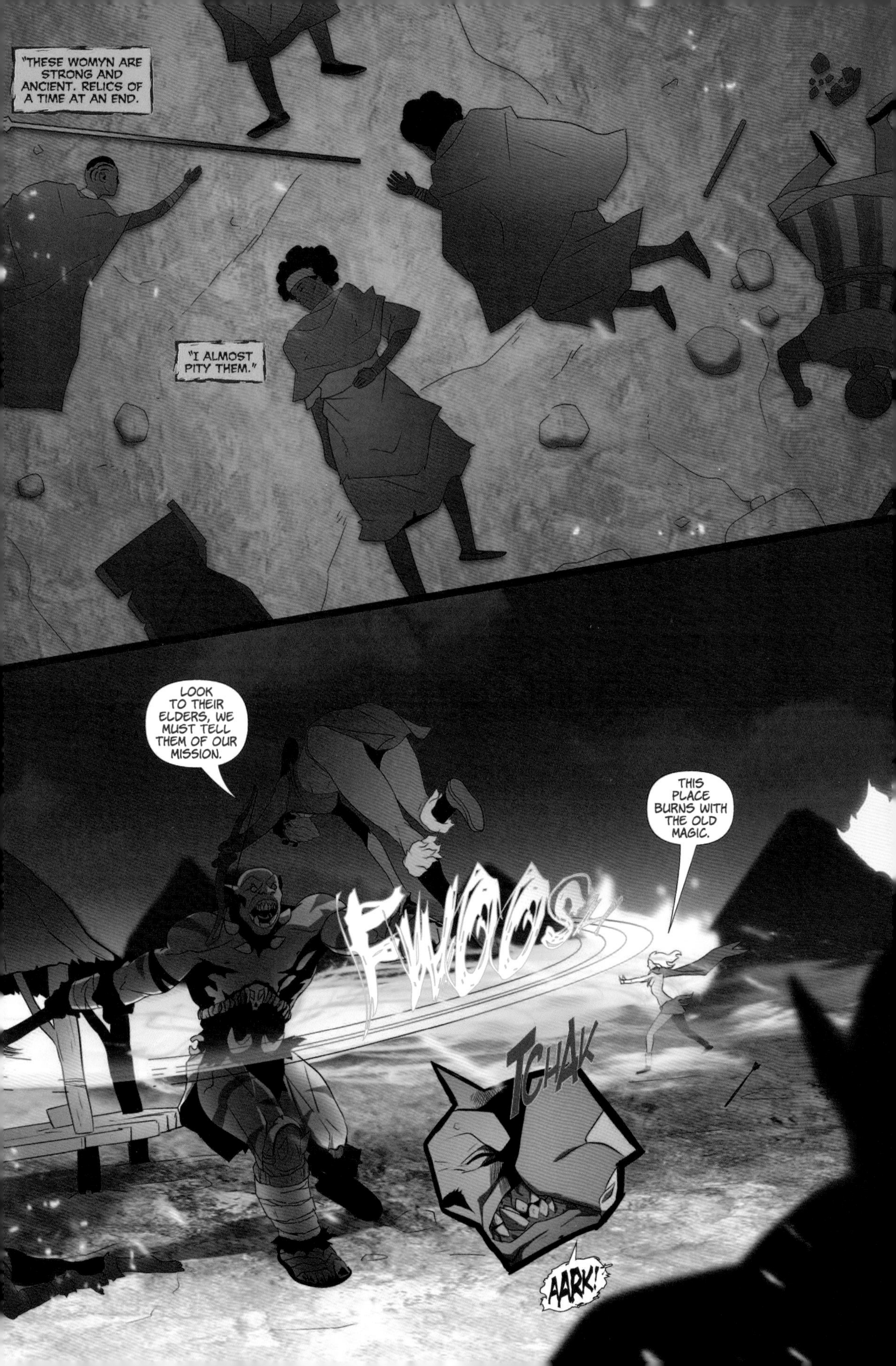
"THESE WOMYN ARE STRONG AND ANCIENT. RELICS OF A TIME AT AN END.
"I ALMOST PITY THEM."
LOOK TO THEIR ELDERS, WE MUST TELL THEM OF OUR MISSION.
THIS PLACE BURNS WITH THE OLD MAGIC.
FWOOSH
TCHAK
AARK!

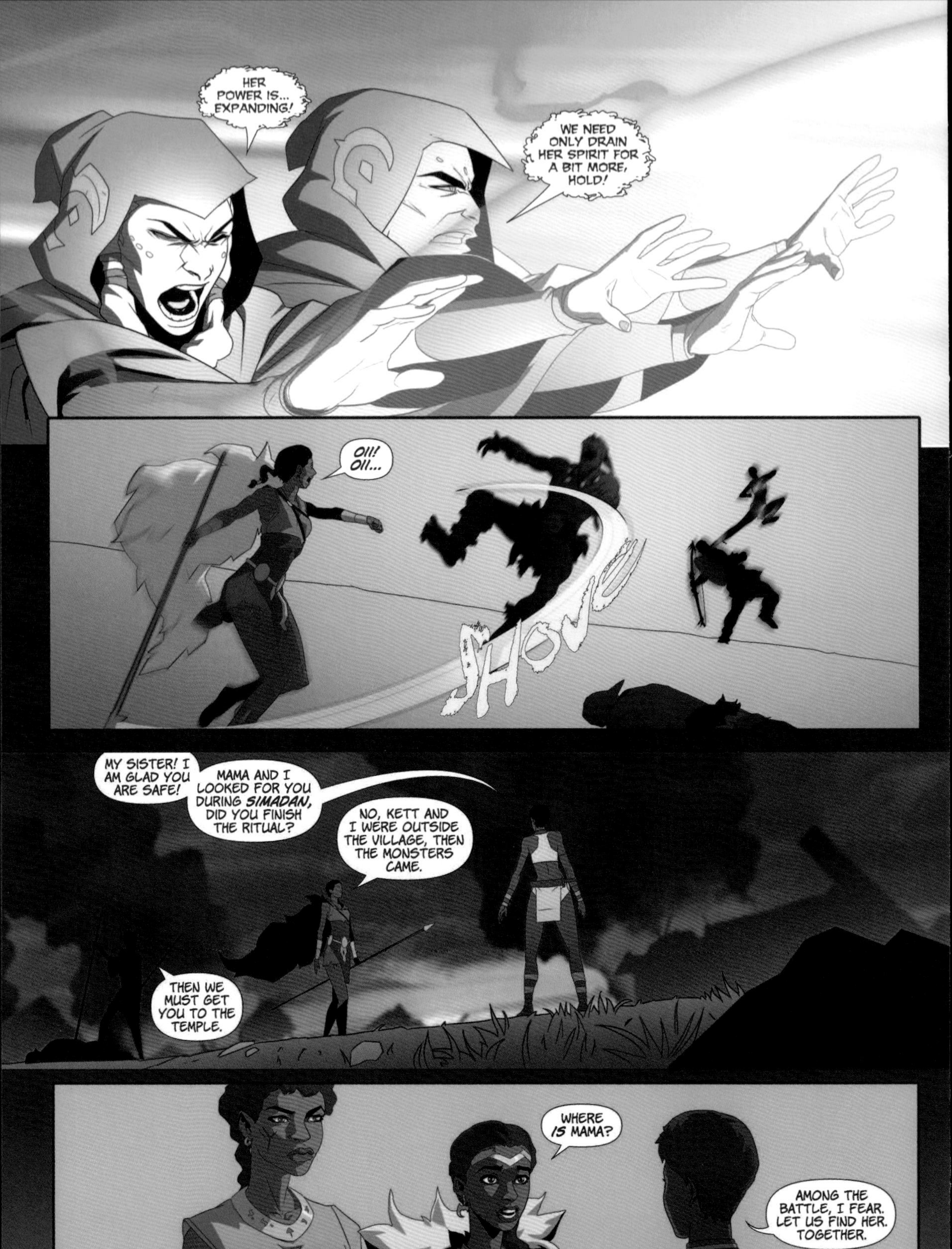
HER POWER IS... EXPANDING!
WE NEED ONLY DRAIN HER SPIRIT FOR A BIT MORE, HOLD!
OII! OII...
SHOVE
MY SISTER! I AM GLAD YOU ARE SAFE!
MAMA AND I LOOKED FOR YOU DURING SIMADAN, DID YOU FINISH THE RITUAL?
NO, KETT AND I WERE OUTSIDE THE VILLAGE, THEN THE MONSTERS CAME.
THEN WE MUST GET YOU TO THE TEMPLE.
WHERE IS MAMA?
AMONG THE BATTLE, I FEAR. LET US FIND HER. TOGETHER.

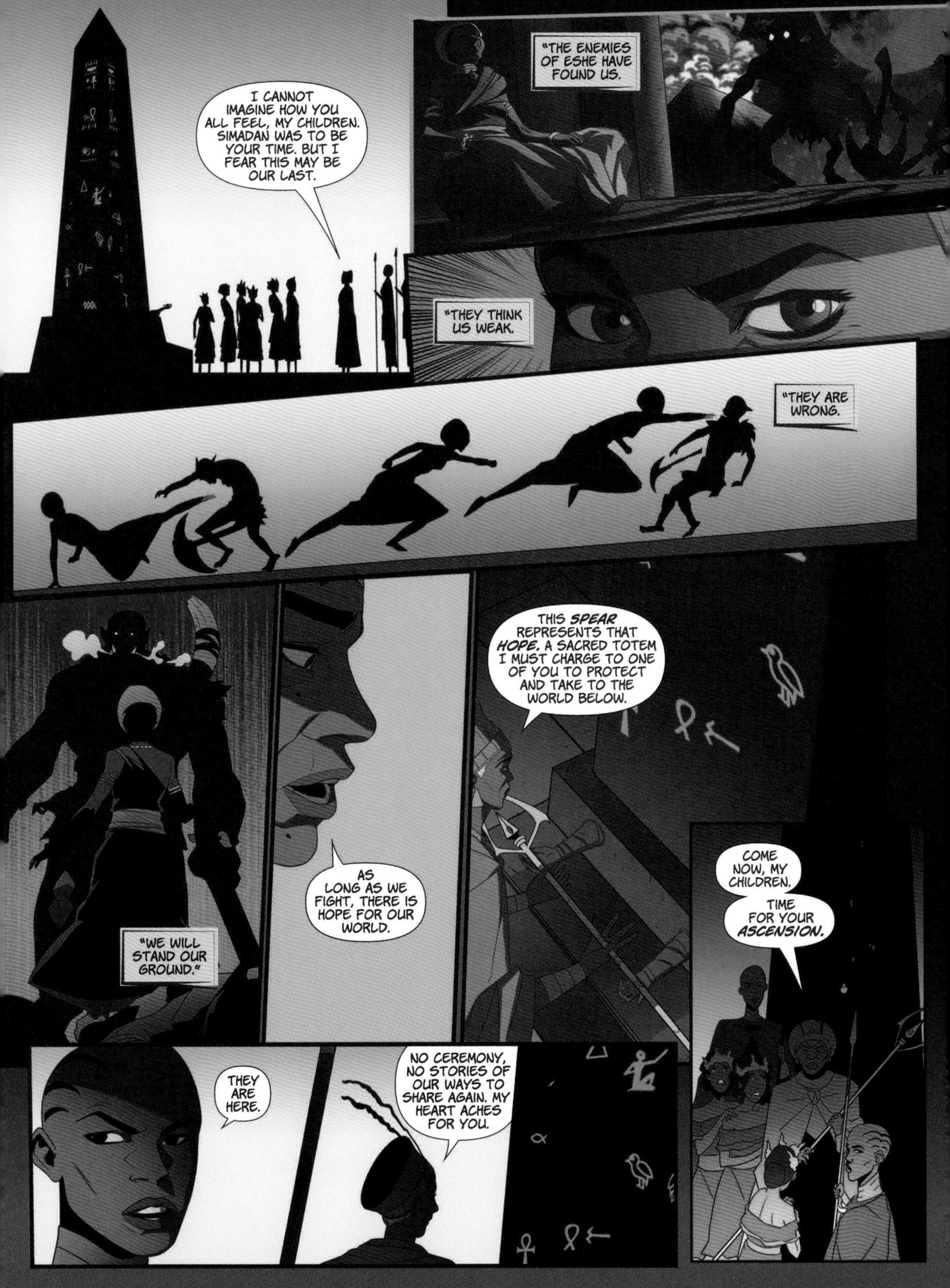
I CANNOT IMAGINE HOW YOU ALL FEEL, MY CHILDREN. SIMADAN WAS TO BE YOUR TIME. BUT I FEAR THIS MAY BE OUR LAST.
"THE ENEMIES OF ESHE HAVE FOUND US.
"THEY THINK US WEAK.
"THEY ARE WRONG.
"WE WILL STAND OUR GROUND."
AS LONG AS WE FIGHT, THERE IS HOPE FOR OUR WORLD.
THIS SPEAR REPRESENTS THAT HOPE. A SACRED TOTEM I MUST CHARGE TO ONE OF YOU TO PROTECT AND TAKE TO THE WORLD BELOW.
THEY ARE HERE.
NO CEREMONY, NO STORIES OF OUR WAYS TO SHARE AGAIN. MY HEART ACHES FOR YOU.
COME NOW, MY CHILDREN.
TIME FOR YOUR ASCENSION.

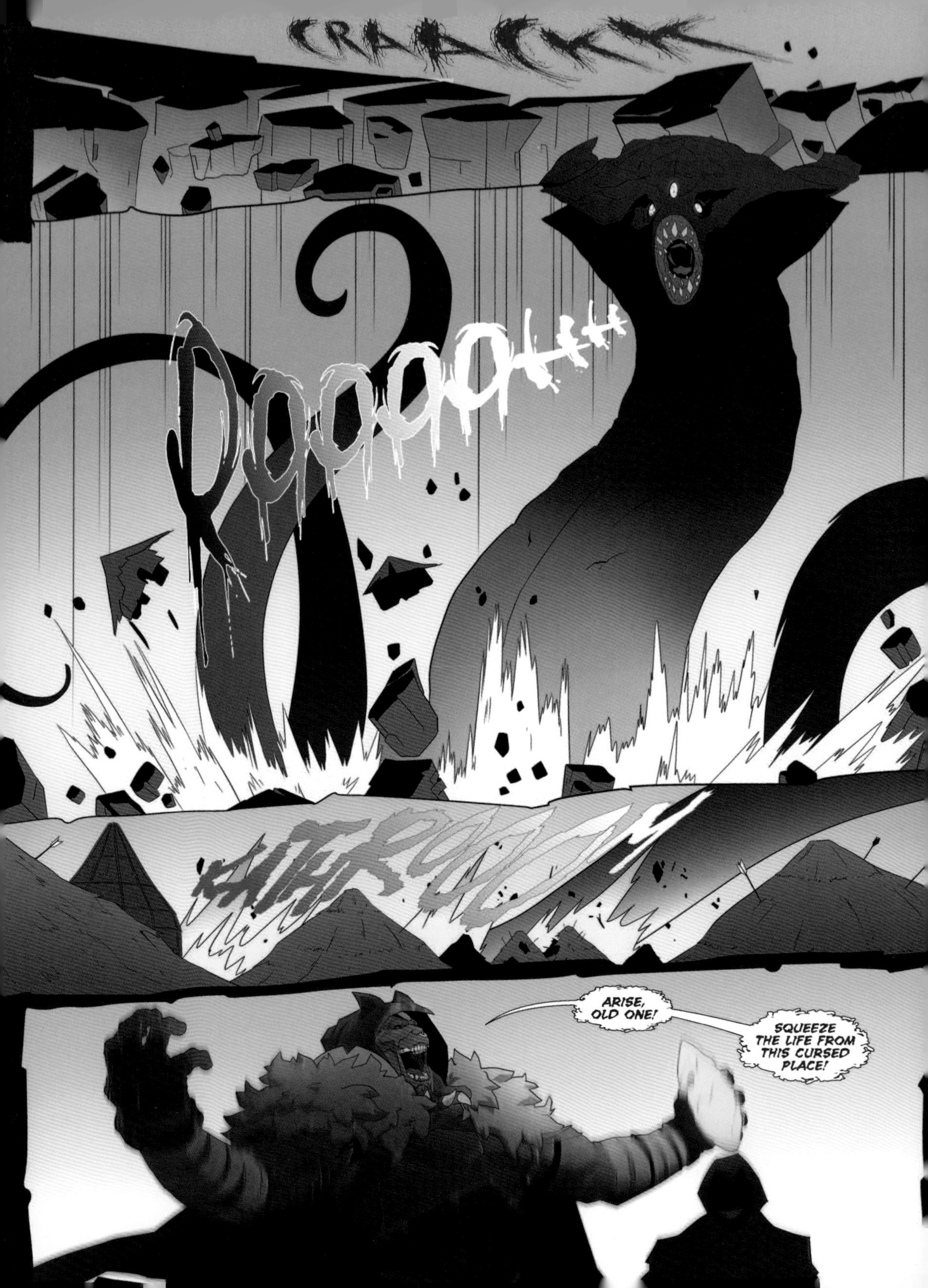
ARISE, OLD ONE!
SQUEEZE THE LIFE FROM THIS CURSED PLACE!

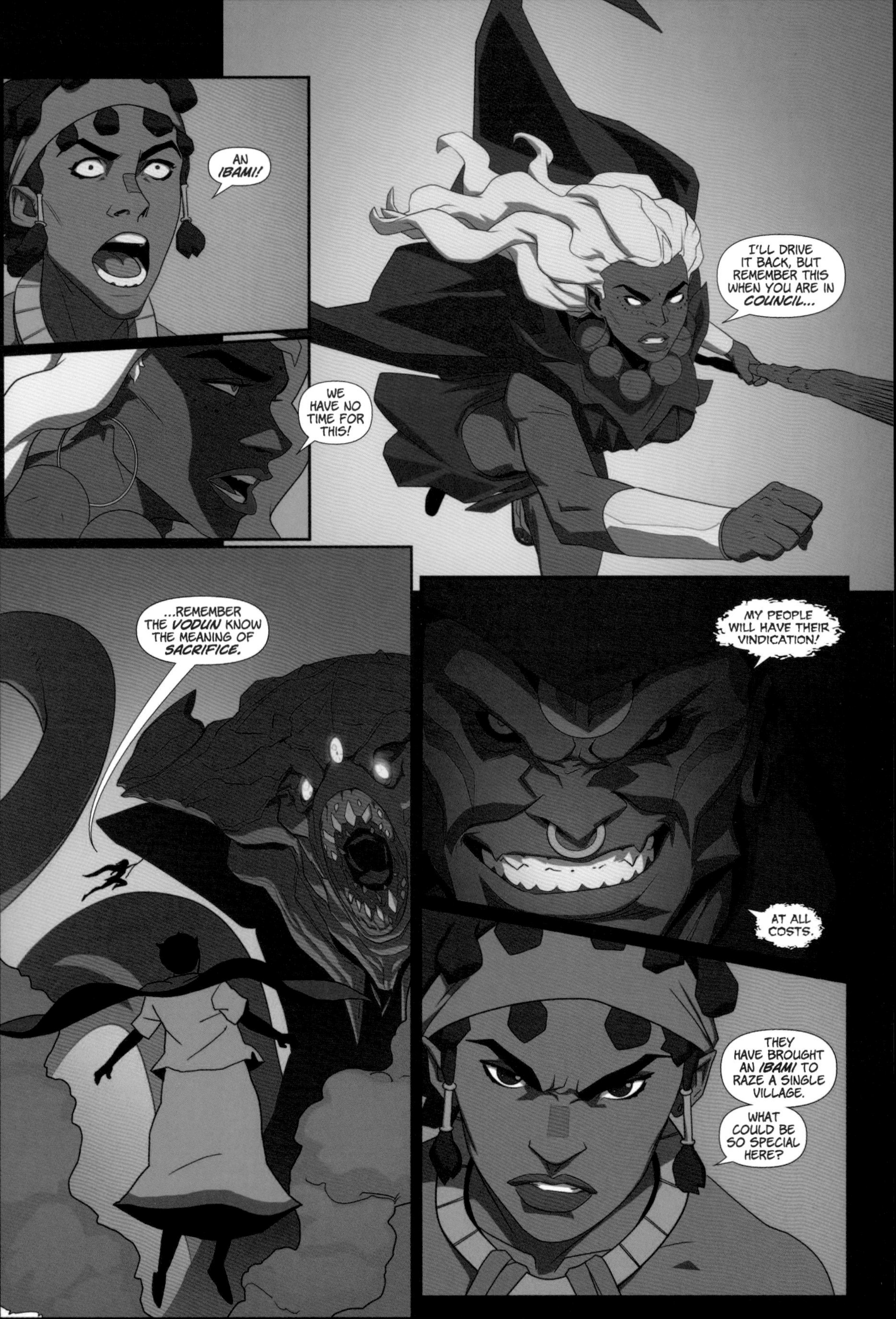
AN IBAMI!
I'LL DRIVE IT BACK, BUT REMEMBER THIS WHEN YOU ARE IN COUNCIL...
WE HAVE NO TIME FOR THIS!
...REMEMBER THE VODUN KNOW THE MEANING OF SACRIFICE.
MY PEOPLE WILL HAVE THEIR VINDICATION!
AT ALL COSTS.
THEY HAVE BROUGHT AN IBAMI TO RAZE A SINGLE VILLAGE.
WHAT COULD BE SO SPECIAL HERE?

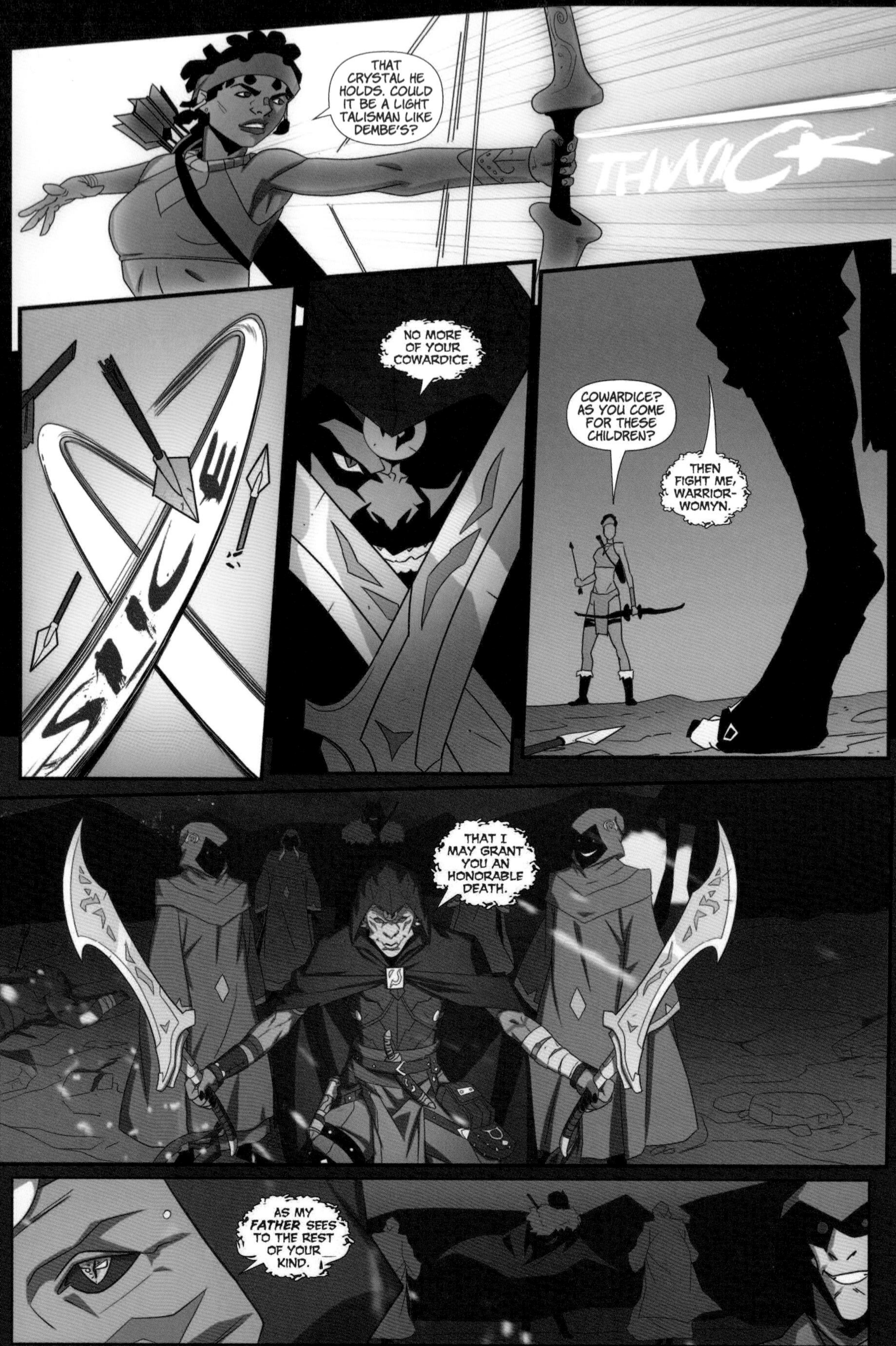
THAT CRYSTAL HE HOLDS. COULD IT BE A LIGHT TALISMAN LIKE DEMBE'S?
THWICK
NO MORE OF YOUR COWARDICE.
COWARDICE? AS YOU COME FOR THESE CHILDREN?
THEN FIGHT ME, WARRIOR-WOMYN.
THAT I MAY GRANT YOU AN HONORABLE DEATH.
AS MY FATHER SEES TO THE REST OF YOUR KIND.

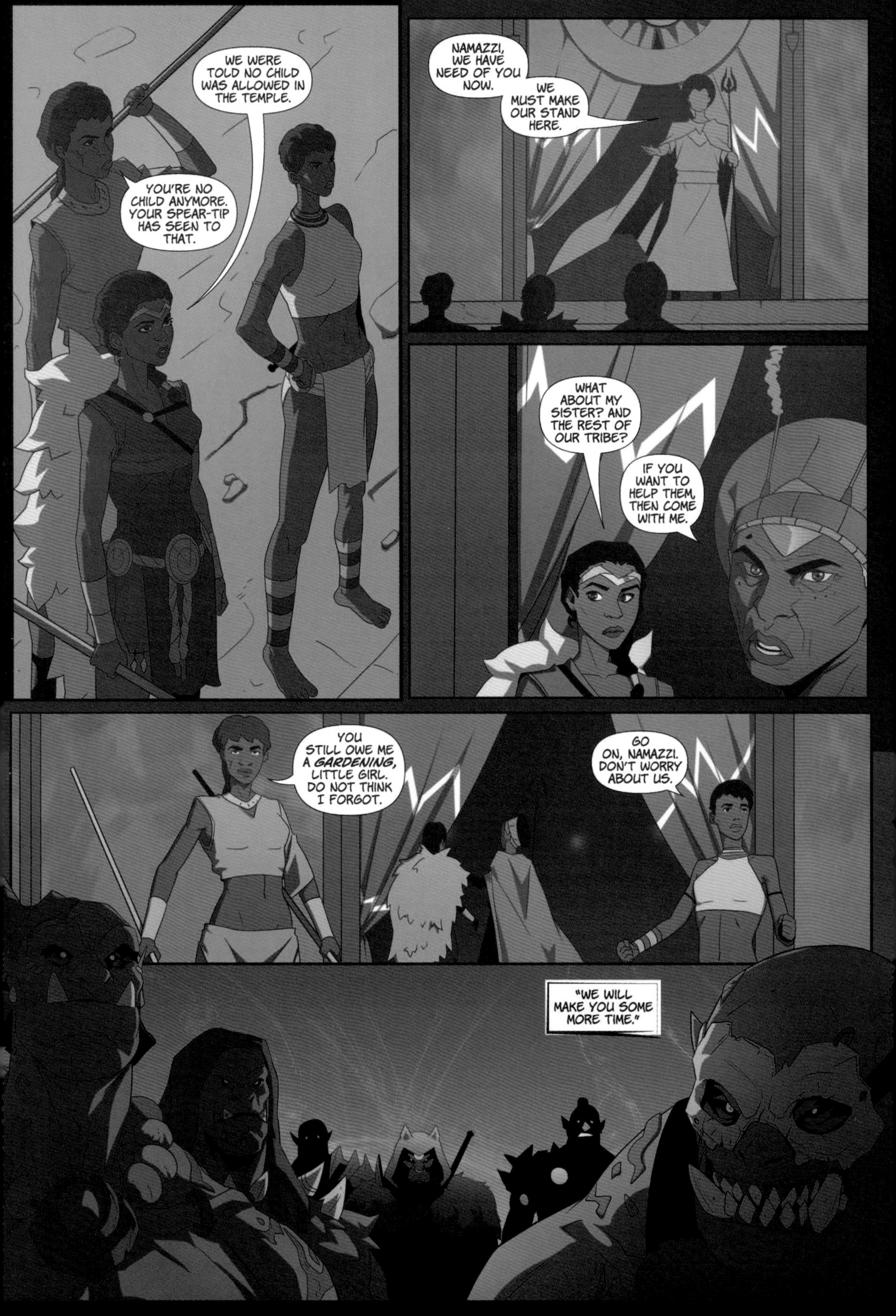
WE WERE TOLD NO CHILD WAS ALLOWED IN THE TEMPLE.
YOU'RE NO CHILD ANYMORE. YOUR SPEAR-TIP HAS SEEN TO THAT.
NAMAZZI, WE HAVE NEED OF YOU NOW.
WE MUST MAKE OUR STAND HERE.
WHAT ABOUT MY SISTER? AND THE REST OF OUR TRIBE?
IF YOU WANT TO HELP THEM, THEN COME WITH ME.
YOU STILL OWE ME A *GARDENING,* LITTLE GIRL. DO NOT THINK I FORGOT.
GO ON, NAMAZZI. DON'T WORRY ABOUT US.
"WE WILL MAKE YOU SOME MORE TIME."

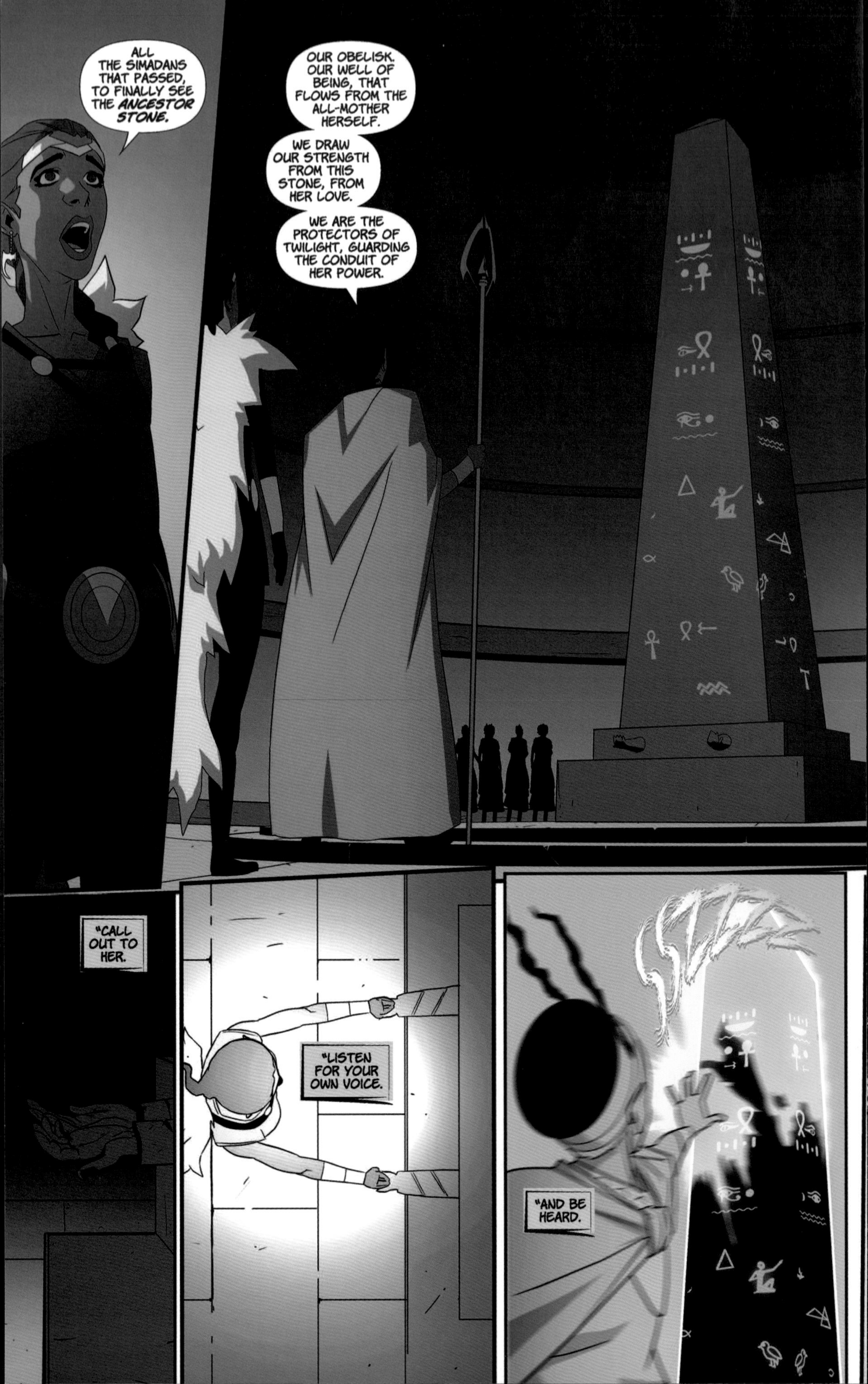
ALL THE SIMADANS THAT PASSED, TO FINALLY SEE THE *ANCESTOR STONE.*
OUR OBELISK. OUR WELL OF BEING, THAT FLOWS FROM THE ALL-MOTHER HERSELF.
WE DRAW OUR STRENGTH FROM THIS STONE, FROM HER LOVE.
WE ARE THE PROTECTORS OF TWILIGHT, GUARDING THE CONDUIT OF HER POWER.
"CALL OUT TO HER.
"LISTEN FOR YOUR OWN VOICE.
"AND BE HEARD.

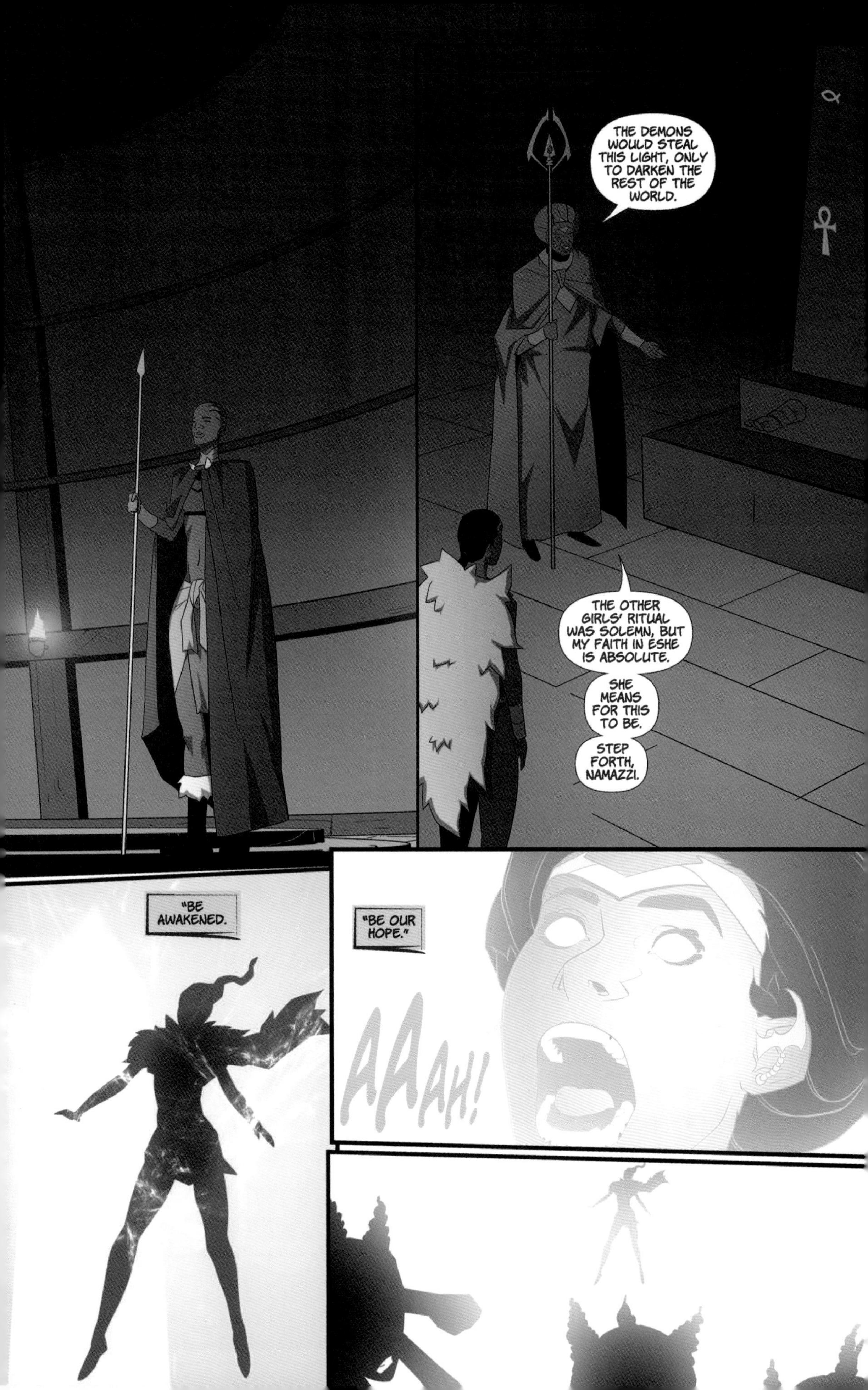
THE DEMONS WOULD STEAL THIS LIGHT, ONLY TO DARKEN THE REST OF THE WORLD.
THE OTHER GIRLS' RITUAL WAS SOLEMN, BUT MY FAITH IN ESHE IS ABSOLUTE.
SHE MEANS FOR THIS TO BE.
STEP FORTH, NAMAZZI.
"BE AWAKENED.
"BE OUR HOPE."
AAAAH!

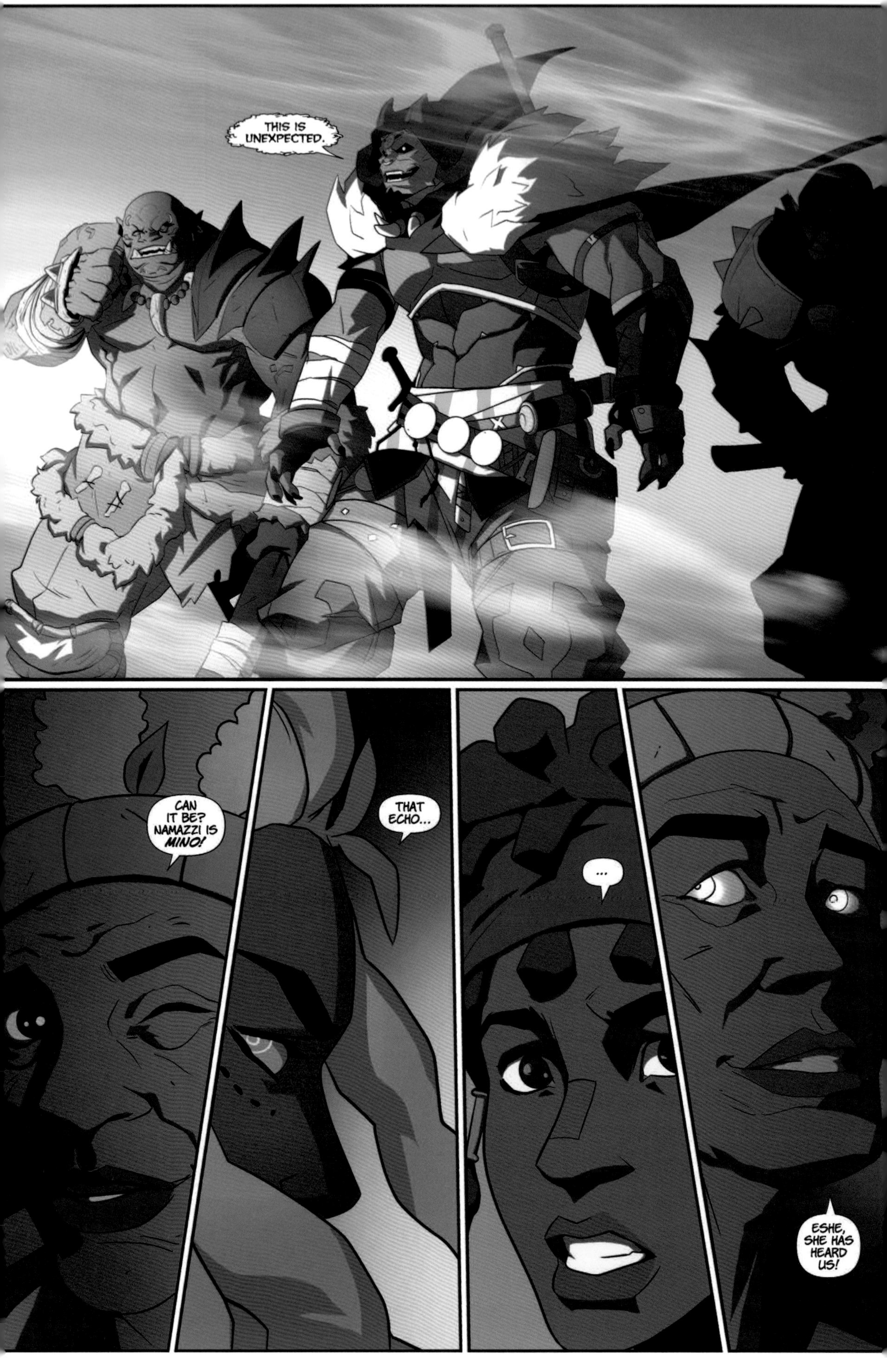
THIS IS UNEXPECTED.
CAN IT BE? NAMAZZI IS *MINO!*
THAT ECHO...
...
ESHE, SHE HAS HEARD US!

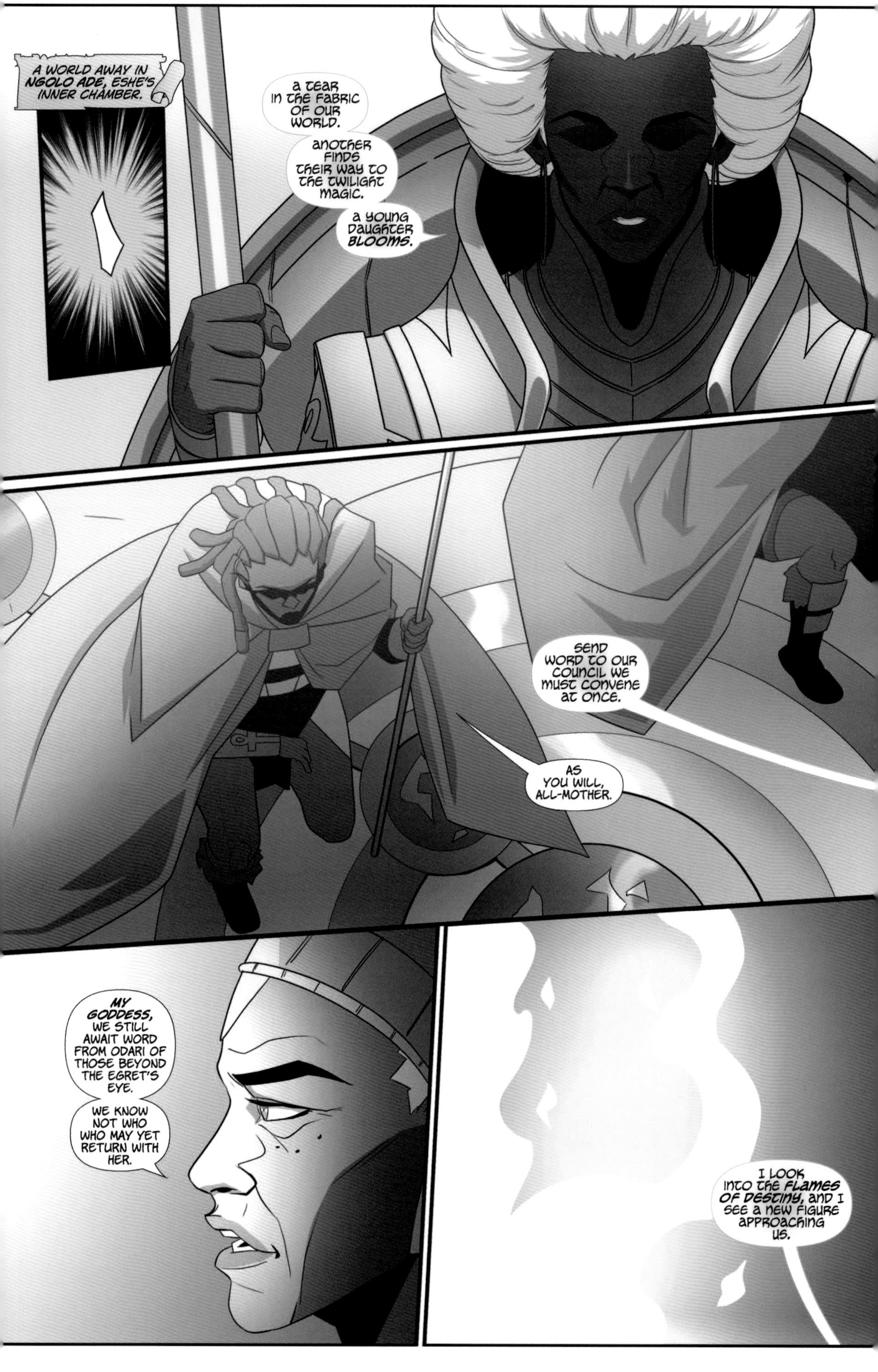
A WORLD AWAY IN NGOLO ADE, ESHE'S INNER CHAMBER.
a tear in the fabric of our world.
another finds their way to the twilight magic.
a young daughter BLOOMS.
send word to our council we must convene at once.
AS YOU WILL, ALL-MOTHER.
MY GODDESS, WE STILL AWAIT WORD FROM ODARI OF THOSE BEYOND THE EGRET'S EYE.
WE KNOW NOT WHO WHO MAY YET RETURN WITH HER.
I look into the FLAMES OF DESTINY, and I see a new figure approaching us.

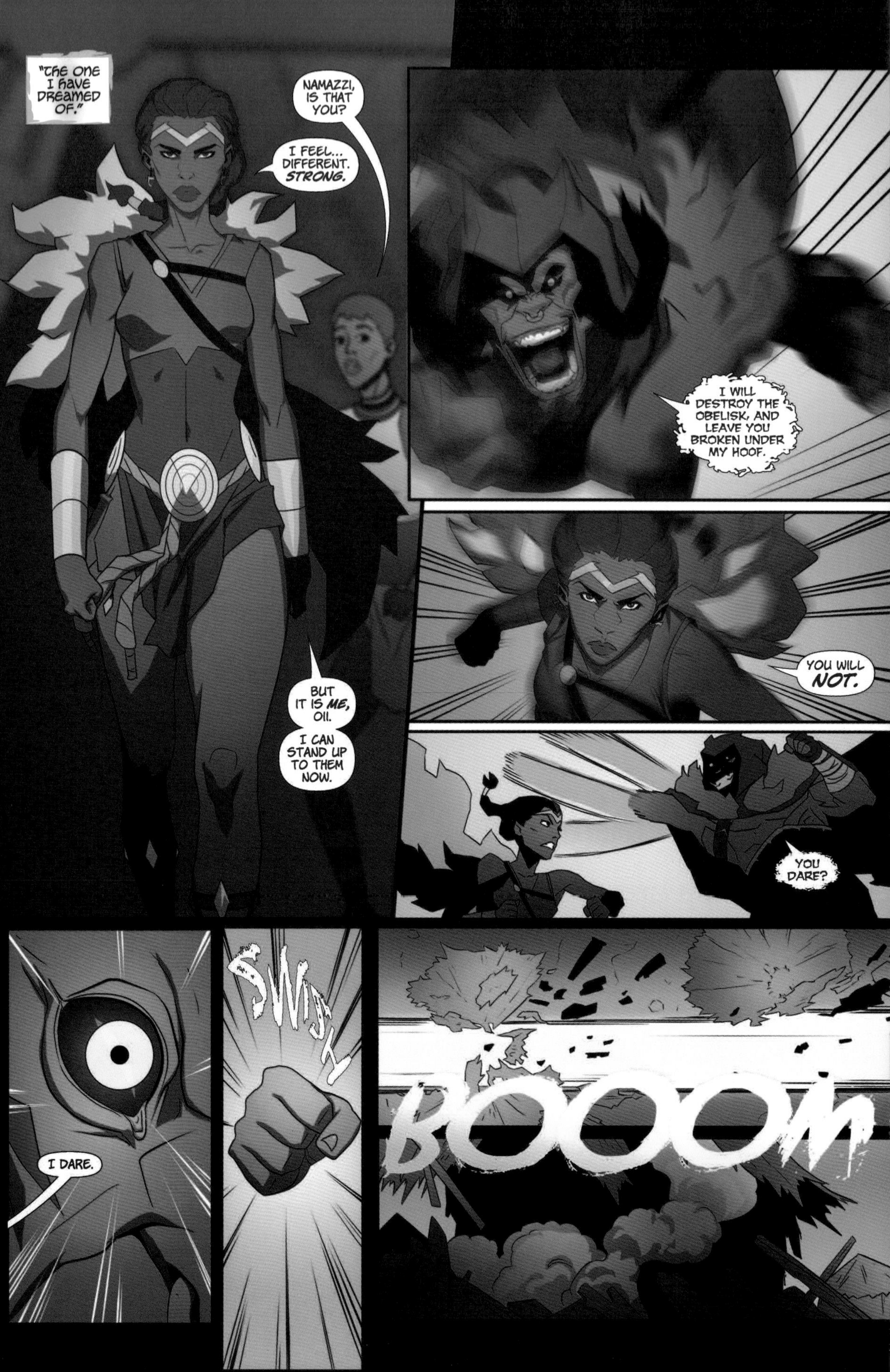
"THE ONE I HAVE DREAMED OF."
NAMAZZI, IS THAT YOU?
I FEEL... DIFFERENT. STRONG.
BUT IT IS ME, OII.
I CAN STAND UP TO THEM NOW.
I WILL DESTROY THE OBELISK, AND LEAVE YOU BROKEN UNDER MY HOOF.
YOU WILL NOT.
YOU DARE?
I DARE.
SWISH
BOOOM

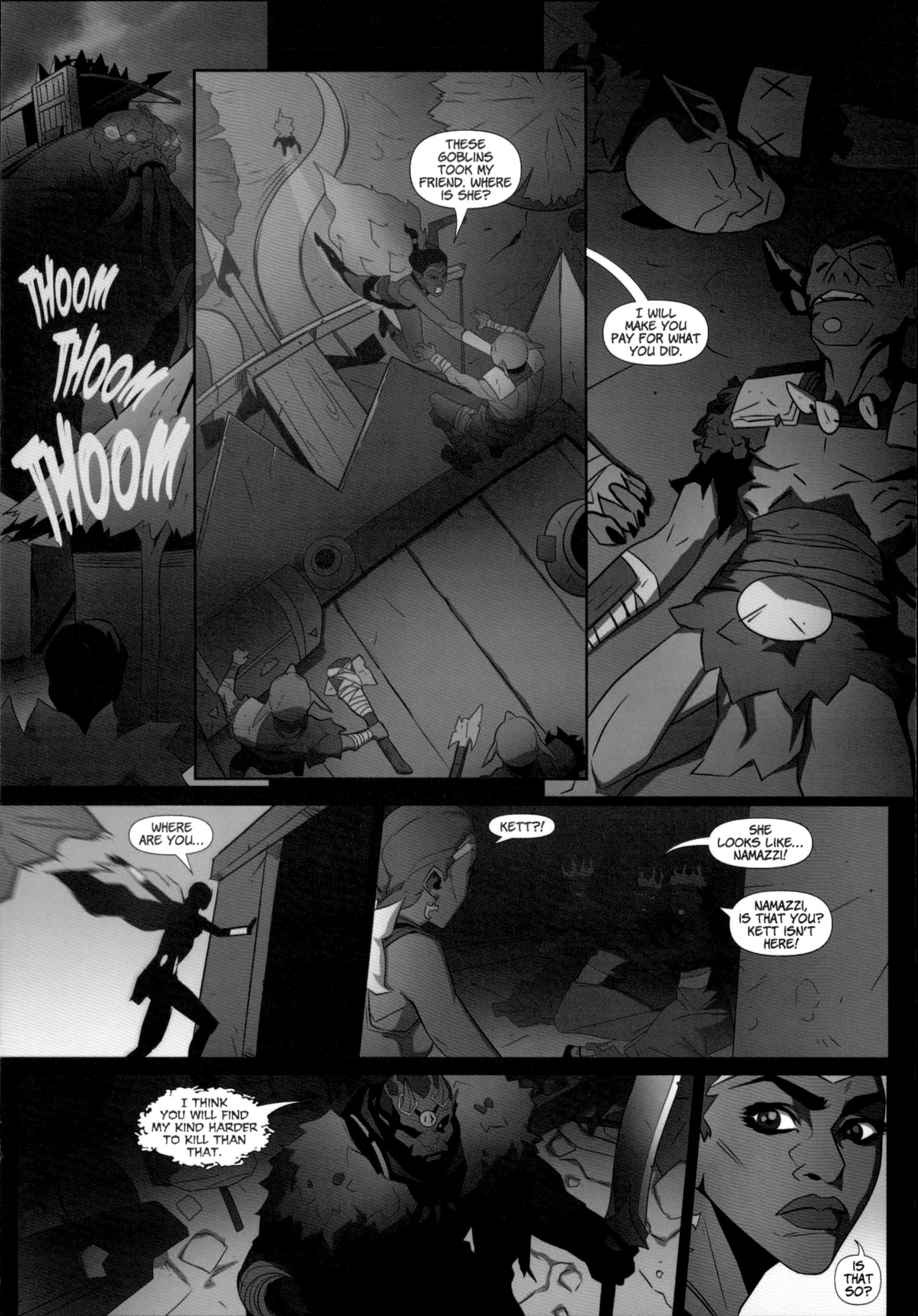
THOOM
THOOM
THOOM
THESE GOBLINS TOOK MY FRIEND. WHERE IS SHE?
I WILL MAKE YOU PAY FOR WHAT YOU DID.
WHERE ARE YOU...
KETT?!
SHE LOOKS LIKE... NAMAZZI!
NAMAZZI, IS THAT YOU? KETT ISN'T HERE!
I THINK YOU WILL FIND MY KIND HARDER TO KILL THAN THAT.
IS THAT SO?

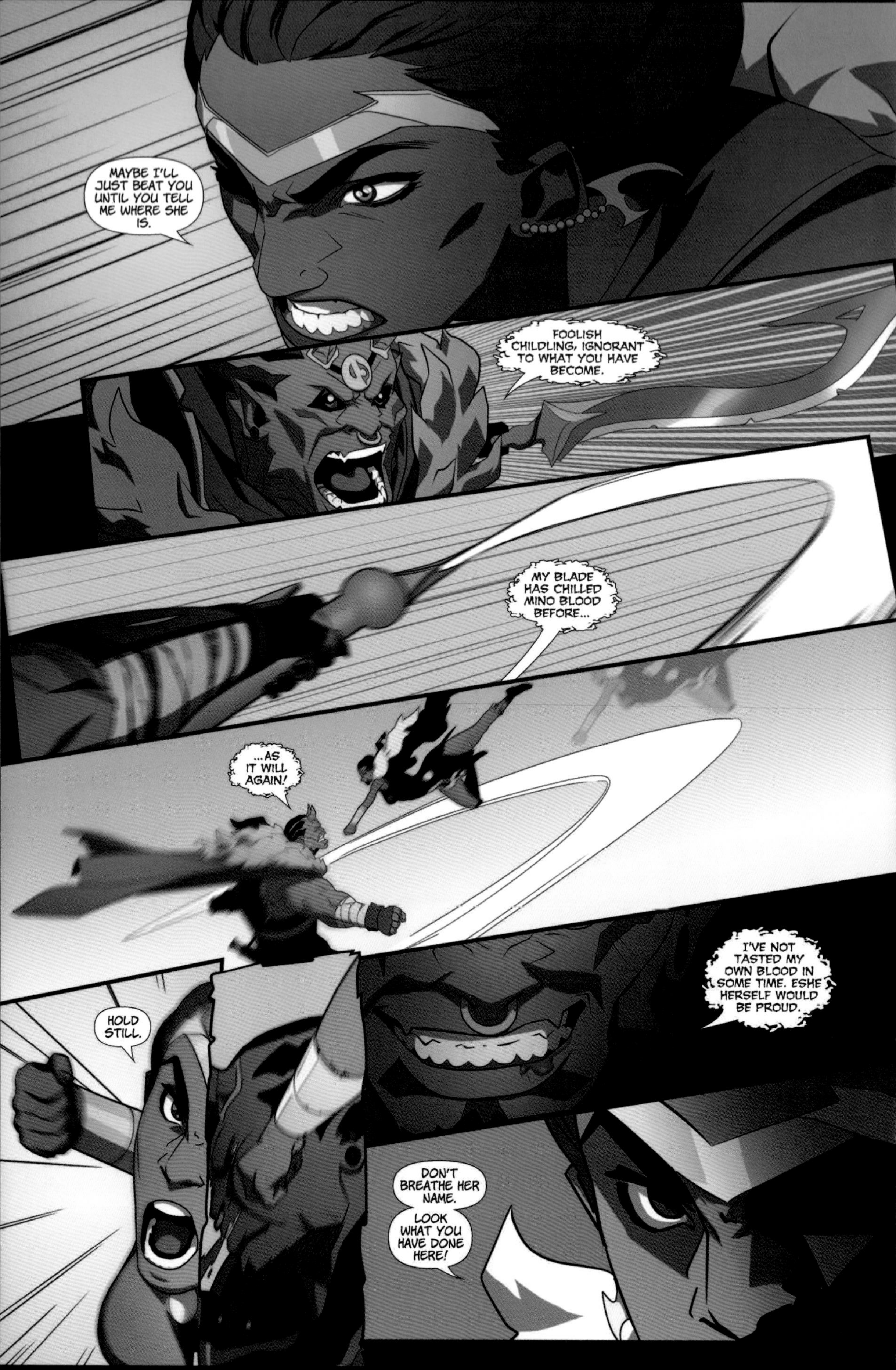
MAYBE I'LL JUST BEAT YOU UNTIL YOU TELL ME WHERE SHE IS.
FOOLISH CHILDLING, IGNORANT TO WHAT YOU HAVE BECOME.
MY BLADE HAS CHILLED MINO BLOOD BEFORE...
...AS IT WILL AGAIN!
I'VE NOT TASTED MY OWN BLOOD IN SOME TIME. ESHE HERSELF WOULD BE PROUD.
HOLD STILL.
DON'T BREATHE HER NAME.
LOOK WHAT YOU HAVE DONE HERE!

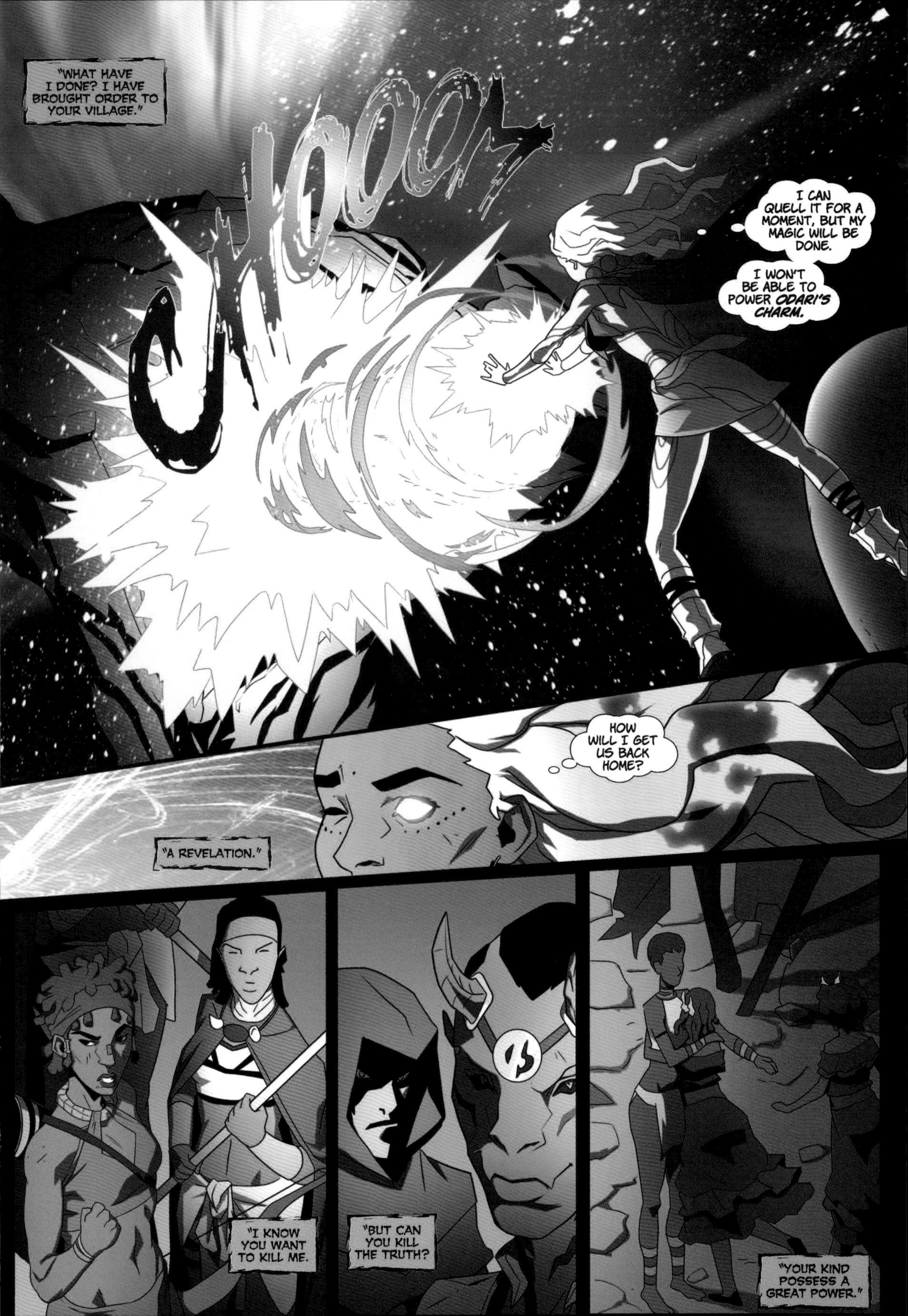
"WHAT HAVE I DONE? I HAVE BROUGHT ORDER TO YOUR VILLAGE."
CHOOOOM
I CAN QUELL IT FOR A MOMENT, BUT MY MAGIC WILL BE DONE.
I WON'T BE ABLE TO POWER *ODARI'S CHARM.*
HOW WILL I GET US BACK HOME?
"A REVELATION."
"I KNOW YOU WANT TO KILL ME.
"BUT CAN YOU KILL THE TRUTH?
"YOUR KIND POSSESS A GREAT POWER."

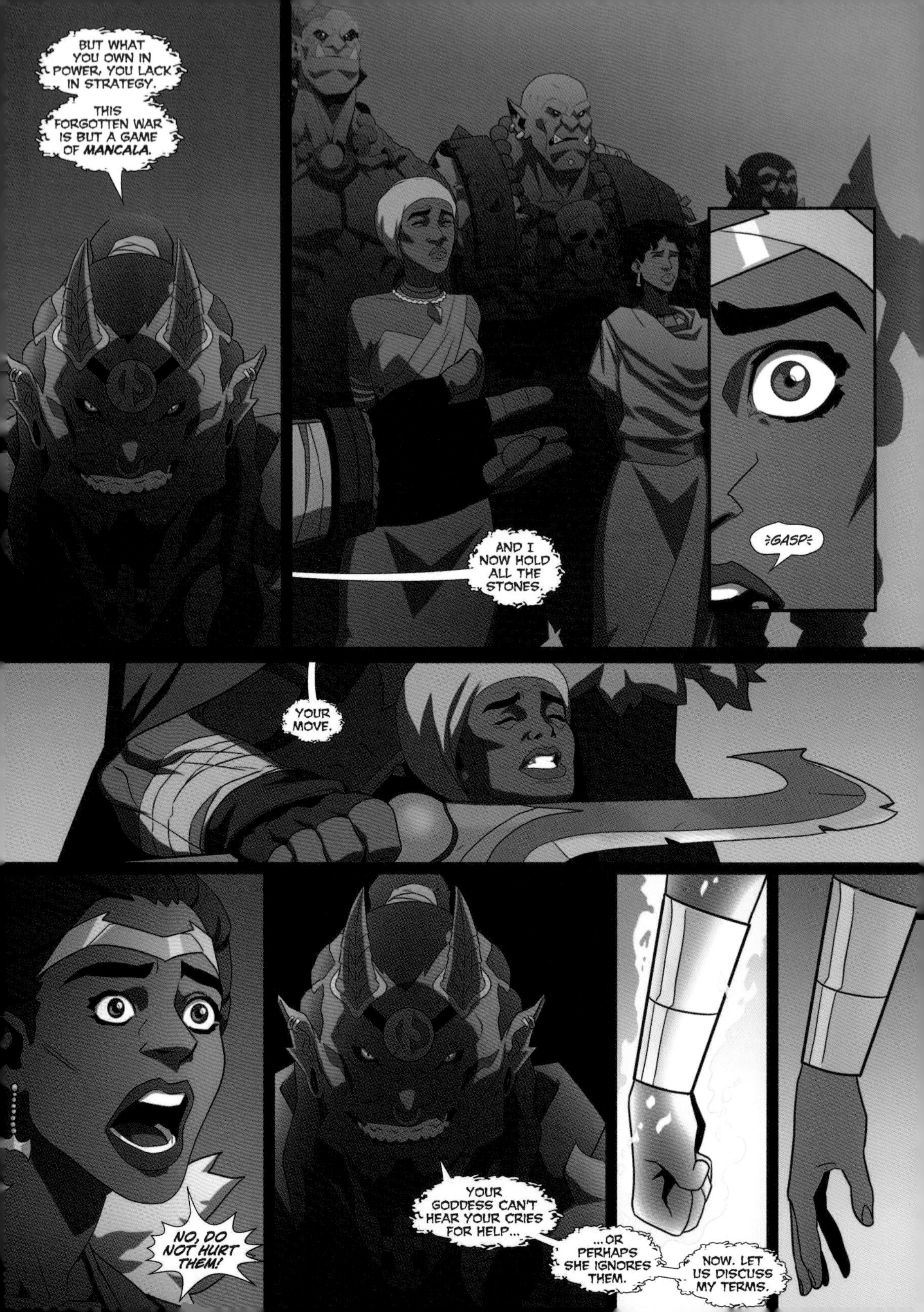
BUT WHAT YOU OWN IN POWER, YOU LACK IN STRATEGY.
THIS FORGOTTEN WAR IS BUT A GAME OF *MANCALA*.
AND I NOW HOLD ALL THE STONES.
GASP
YOUR MOVE.
NO, DO NOT HURT THEM!
YOUR GODDESS CAN'T HEAR YOUR CRIES FOR HELP...
...OR PERHAPS SHE IGNORES THEM.
NOW. LET US DISCUSS MY TERMS.

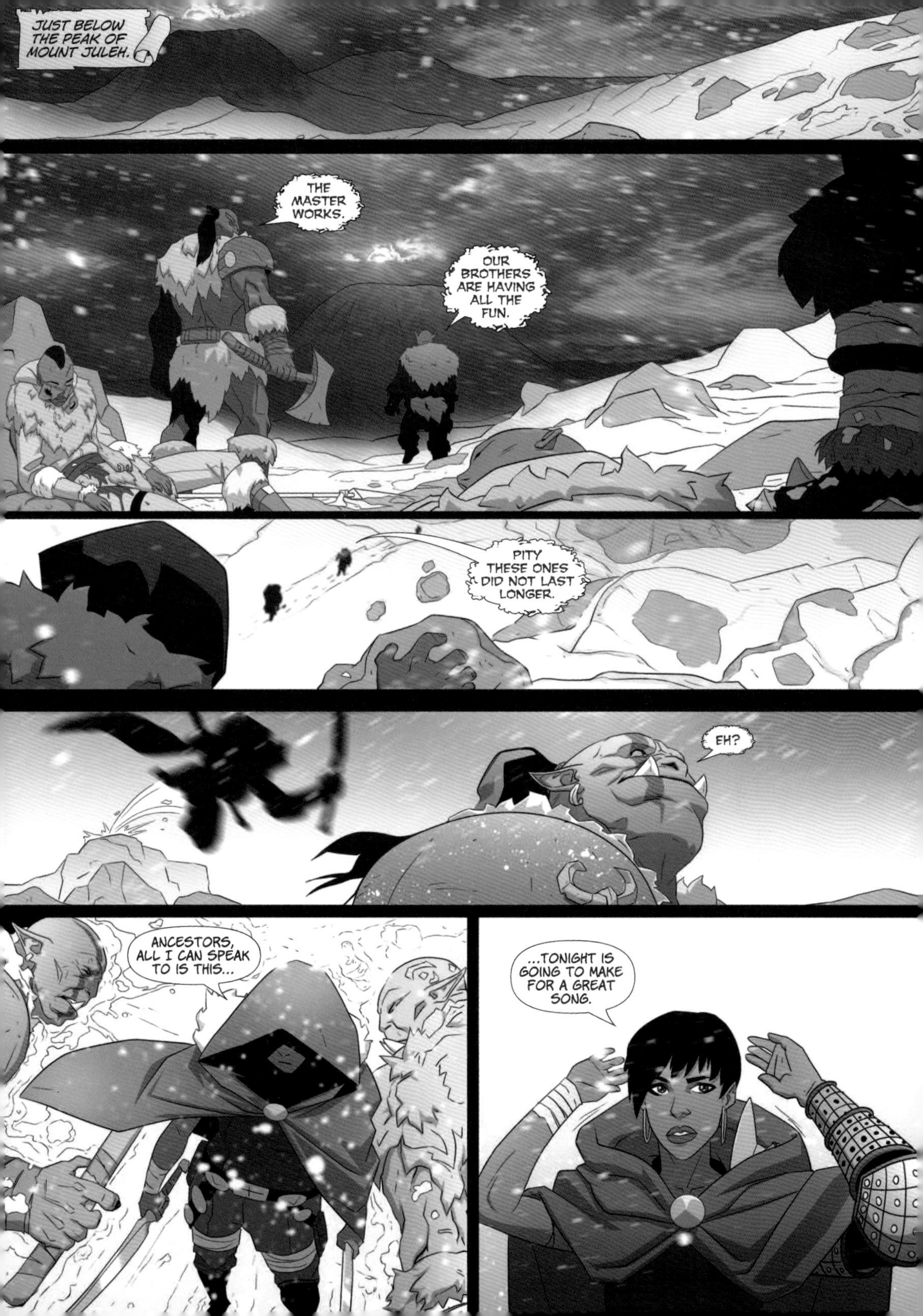
JUST BELOW THE PEAK OF MOUNT JULEH.
THE MASTER WORKS.
OUR BROTHERS ARE HAVING ALL THE FUN.
PITY THESE ONES DID NOT LAST LONGER.
EH?
ANCESTORS, ALL I CAN SPEAK TO IS THIS...
...TONIGHT IS GOING TO MAKE FOR A GREAT SONG.

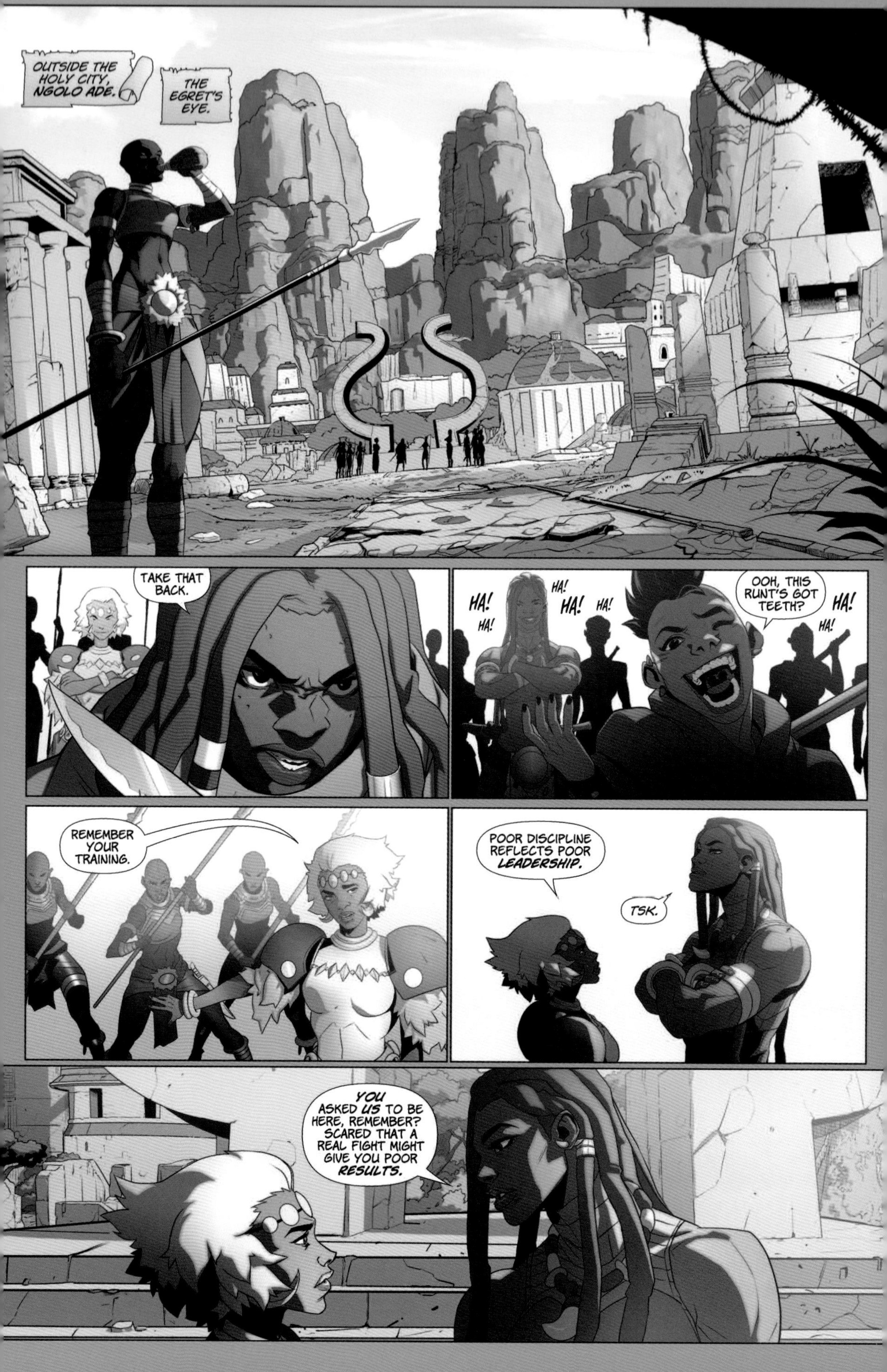
OUTSIDE THE HOLY CITY, NGOLO ADE.
THE EGRET'S EYE.
TAKE THAT BACK.
HA! HA! HA! HA! HA!
OOH, THIS RUNT'S GOT TEETH?
HA! HA!
REMEMBER YOUR TRAINING.
POOR DISCIPLINE REFLECTS POOR LEADERSHIP.
TSK.
YOU ASKED US TO BE HERE, REMEMBER? SCARED THAT A REAL FIGHT MIGHT GIVE YOU POOR RESULTS.

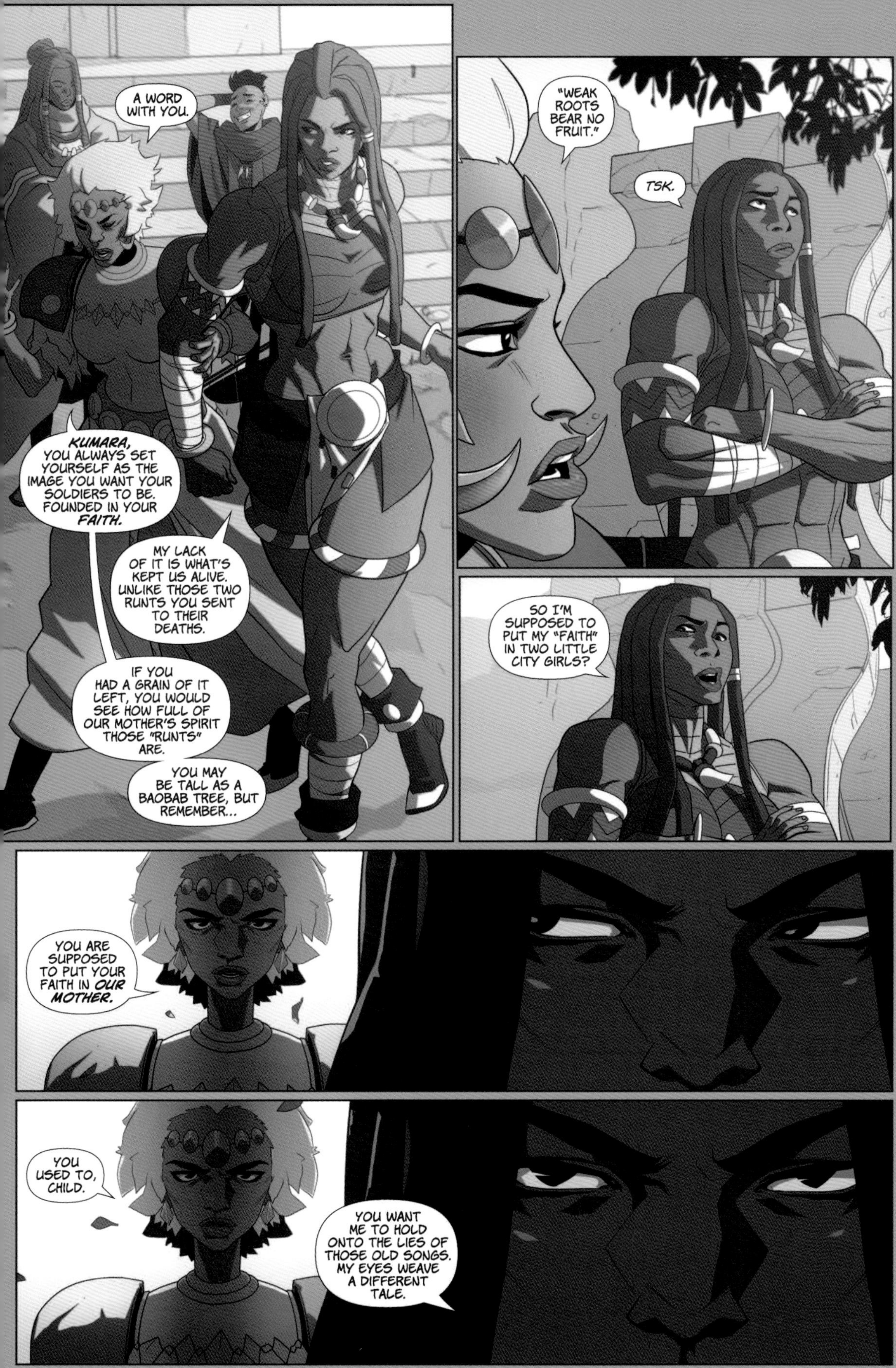
A WORD WITH YOU.
KUMARA, YOU ALWAYS SET YOURSELF AS THE IMAGE YOU WANT YOUR SOLDIERS TO BE. FOUNDED IN YOUR FAITH.
MY LACK OF IT IS WHAT'S KEPT US ALIVE. UNLIKE THOSE TWO RUNTS YOU SENT TO THEIR DEATHS.
IF YOU HAD A GRAIN OF IT LEFT, YOU WOULD SEE HOW FULL OF OUR MOTHER'S SPIRIT THOSE "RUNTS" ARE.
YOU MAY BE TALL AS A BAOBAB TREE, BUT REMEMBER...
"WEAK ROOTS BEAR NO FRUIT."
TSK.
SO I'M SUPPOSED TO PUT MY "FAITH" IN TWO LITTLE CITY GIRLS?
YOU ARE SUPPOSED TO PUT YOUR FAITH IN OUR MOTHER.
YOU USED TO, CHILD.
YOU WANT ME TO HOLD ONTO THE LIES OF THOSE OLD SONGS. MY EYES WEAVE A DIFFERENT TALE.

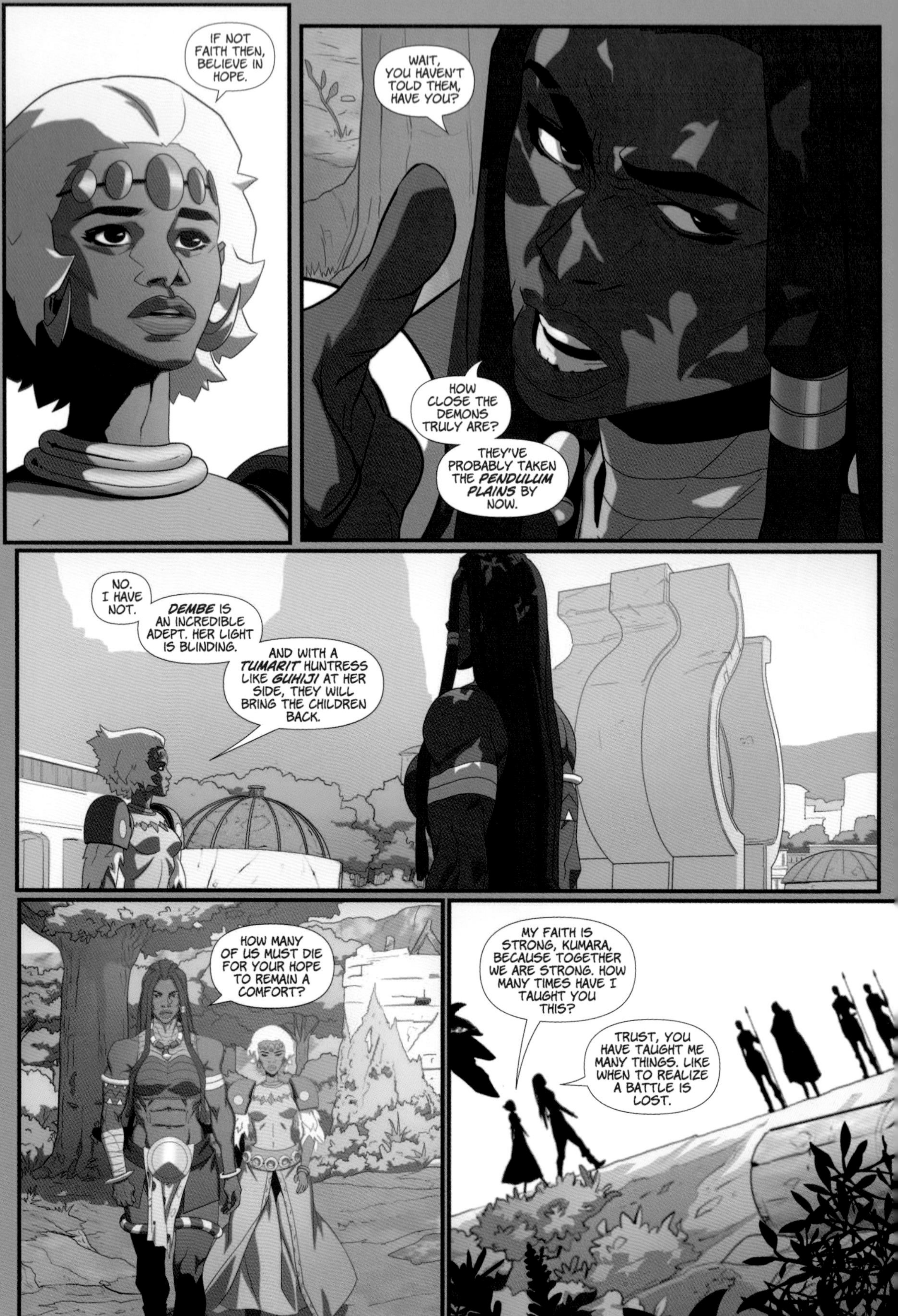
IF NOT FAITH THEN, BELIEVE IN HOPE.
WAIT, YOU HAVEN'T TOLD THEM, HAVE YOU?
HOW CLOSE THE DEMONS TRULY ARE?
THEY'VE PROBABLY TAKEN THE PENDULUM PLAINS BY NOW.
NO. I HAVE NOT.
DEMBE IS AN INCREDIBLE ADEPT. HER LIGHT IS BLINDING.
AND WITH A TUMARIT HUNTRESS LIKE GUHIJI AT HER SIDE, THEY WILL BRING THE CHILDREN BACK.
HOW MANY OF US MUST DIE FOR YOUR HOPE TO REMAIN A COMFORT?
MY FAITH IS STRONG, KUMARA, BECAUSE TOGETHER WE ARE STRONG. HOW MANY TIMES HAVE I TAUGHT YOU THIS?
TRUST, YOU HAVE TAUGHT ME MANY THINGS. LIKE WHEN TO REALIZE A BATTLE IS LOST.

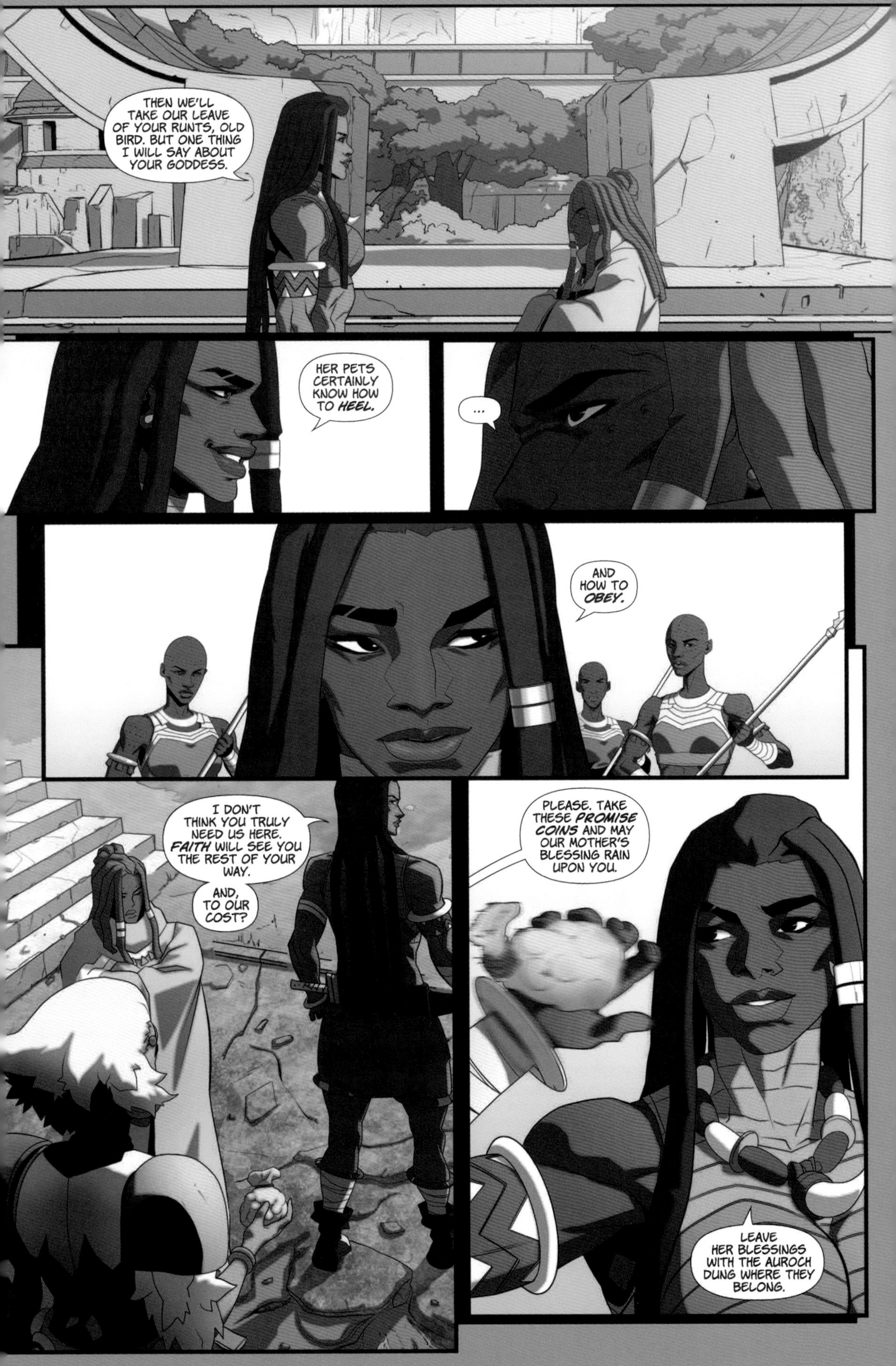
THEN WE'LL TAKE OUR LEAVE OF YOUR RUNTS, OLD BIRD. BUT ONE THING I WILL SAY ABOUT YOUR GODDESS.
HER PETS CERTAINLY KNOW HOW TO *HEEL.*
...
AND HOW TO *OBEY.*
I DON'T THINK YOU TRULY NEED US HERE. *FAITH* WILL SEE YOU THE REST OF YOUR WAY.
AND, TO OUR COST?
PLEASE. TAKE THESE *PROMISE COINS* AND MAY OUR MOTHER'S BLESSING RAIN UPON YOU.
LEAVE HER BLESSINGS WITH THE AUROCH DUNG WHERE THEY BELONG.

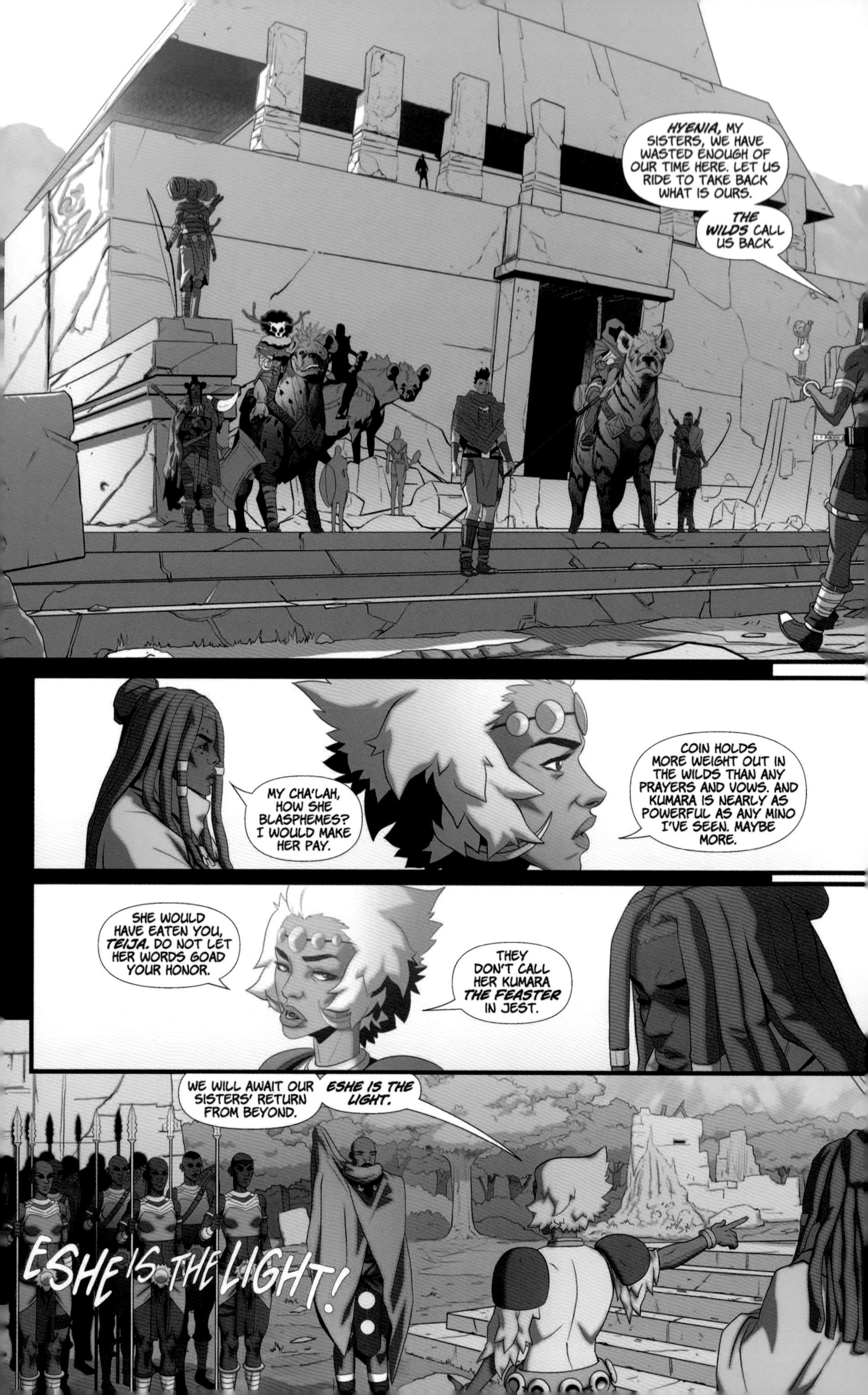

HYENIA, MY SISTERS, WE HAVE WASTED ENOUGH OF OUR TIME HERE. LET US RIDE TO TAKE BACK WHAT IS OURS.
THE WILDS CALL US BACK.
MY CHA'LAH, HOW SHE BLASPHEMES? I WOULD MAKE HER PAY.
COIN HOLDS MORE WEIGHT OUT IN THE WILDS THAN ANY PRAYERS AND VOWS. AND KUMARA IS NEARLY AS POWERFUL AS ANY MINO I'VE SEEN. MAYBE MORE.
SHE WOULD HAVE EATEN YOU, TEIJA. DO NOT LET HER WORDS GOAD YOUR HONOR.
THEY DON'T CALL HER KUMARA THE FEASTER IN JEST.
WE WILL AWAIT OUR SISTERS' RETURN FROM BEYOND.
ESHE IS THE LIGHT.
ESHE IS THE LIGHT!

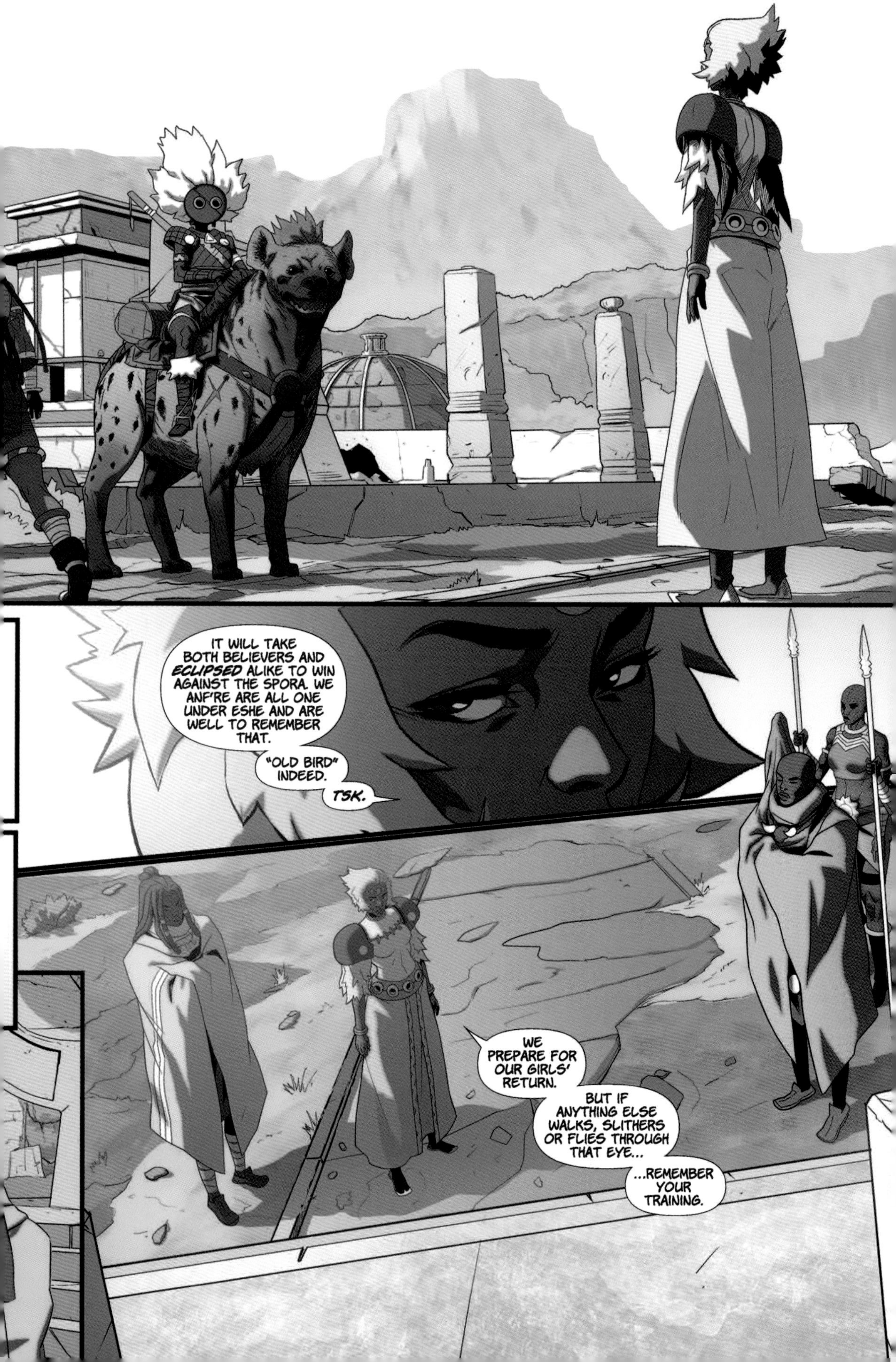
IT WILL TAKE BOTH BELIEVERS AND *ECLIPSED* ALIKE TO WIN AGAINST THE SPORA. WE ANF'RE ARE ALL ONE UNDER ESHE AND ARE WELL TO REMEMBER THAT.
"OLD BIRD" INDEED.
TSK.
WE PREPARE FOR OUR GIRLS' RETURN.
BUT IF ANYTHING ELSE WALKS, SLITHERS OR FLIES THROUGH THAT EYE...
...REMEMBER YOUR TRAINING.

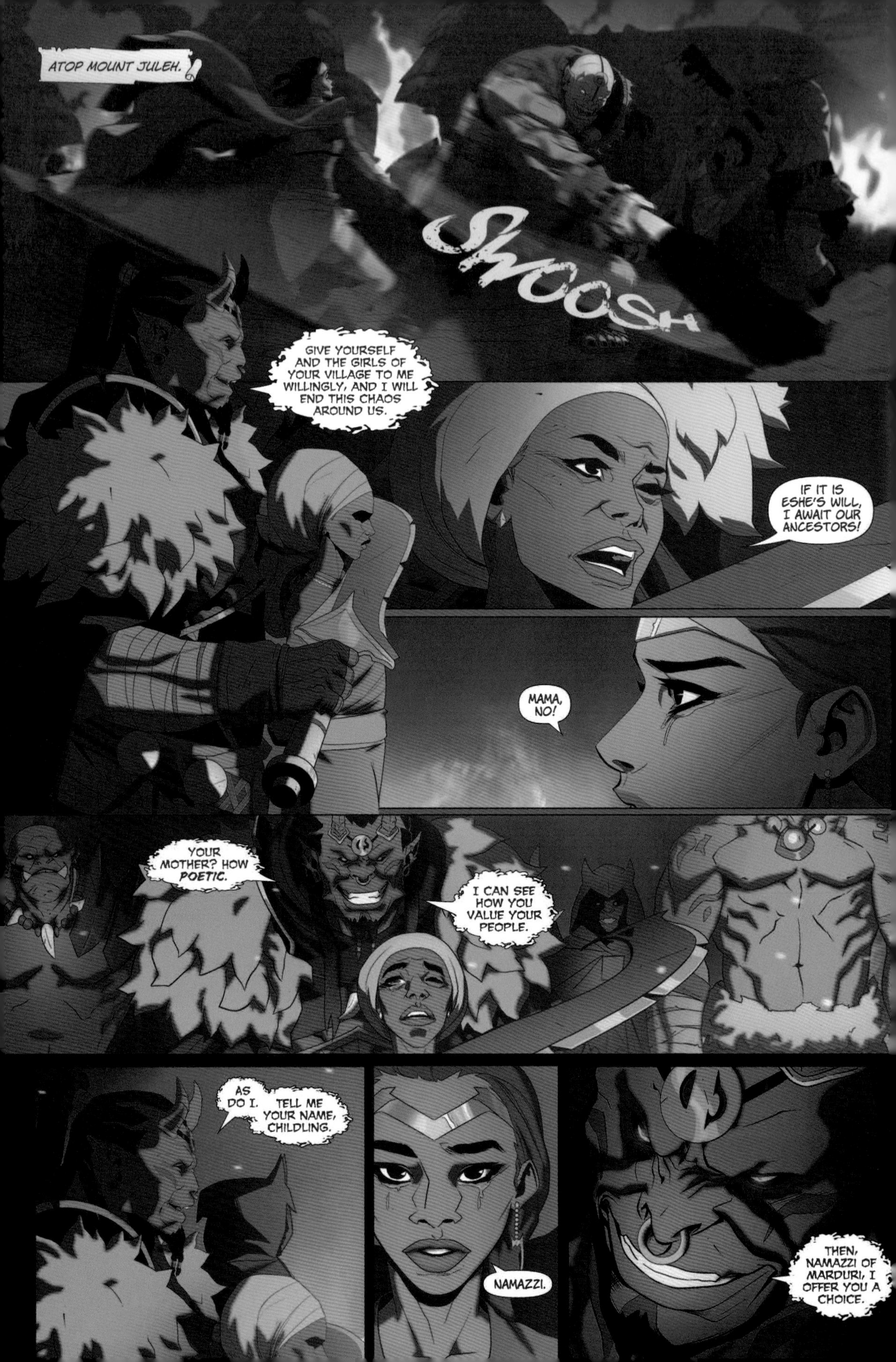
ATOP MOUNT JULEH.
SWOOSH
GIVE YOURSELF AND THE GIRLS OF YOUR VILLAGE TO ME WILLINGLY, AND I WILL END THIS CHAOS AROUND US.
IF IT IS ESHE'S WILL, I AWAIT OUR ANCESTORS!
MAMA, NO!
YOUR MOTHER? HOW POETIC.
I CAN SEE HOW YOU VALUE YOUR PEOPLE.
AS DO I.
TELL ME YOUR NAME, CHILDLING.
NAMAZZI.
THEN, NAMAZZI OF MARDURI, I OFFER YOU A CHOICE.

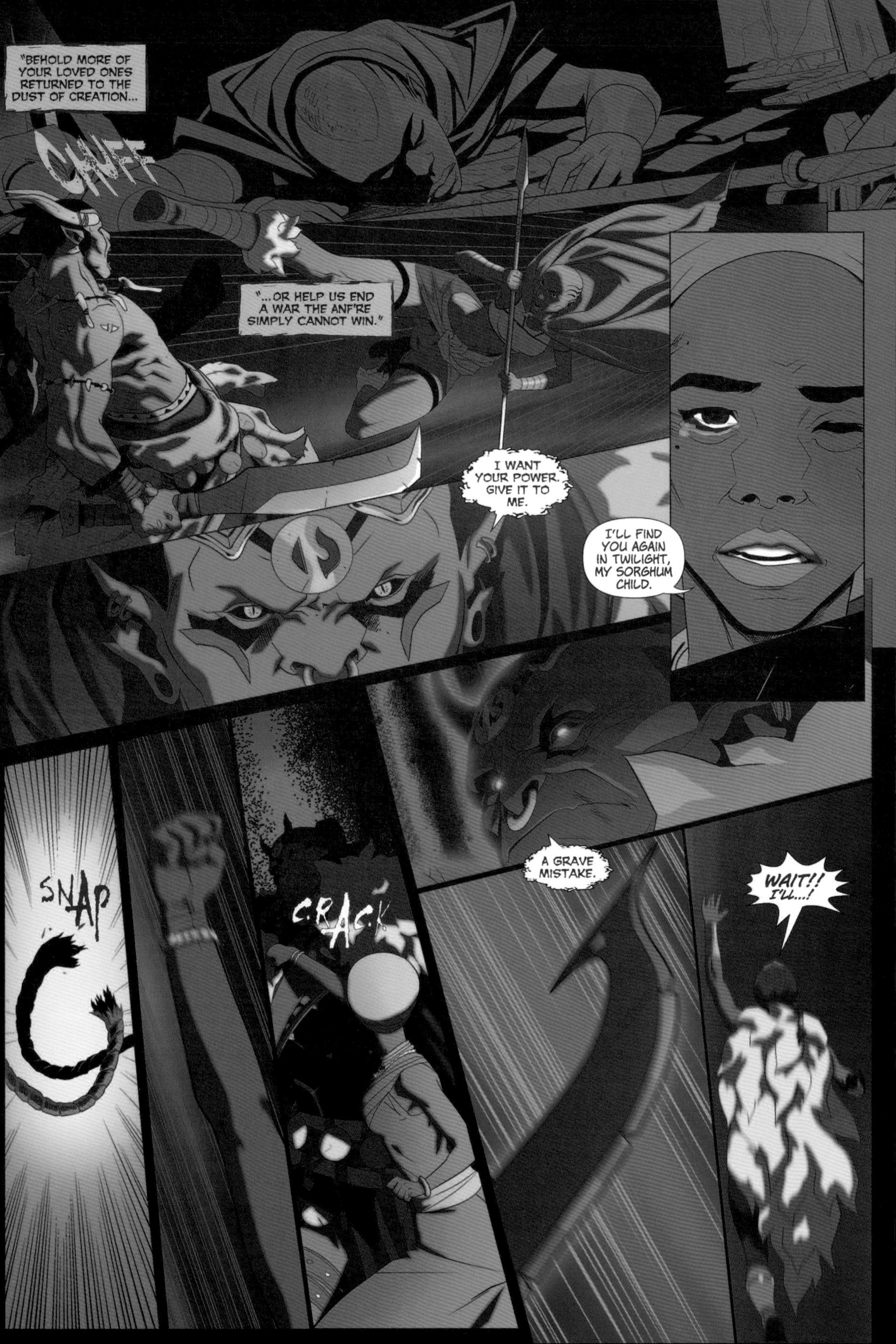
"BEHOLD MORE OF YOUR LOVED ONES RETURNED TO THE DUST OF CREATION...
CHFF
"...OR HELP US END A WAR THE ANF'RE SIMPLY CANNOT WIN."
I WANT YOUR POWER. GIVE IT TO ME.
I'LL FIND YOU AGAIN IN TWILIGHT, MY SORGHUM CHILD.
A GRAVE MISTAKE.
SNAP
CRACK
WAIT!! I'LL...!

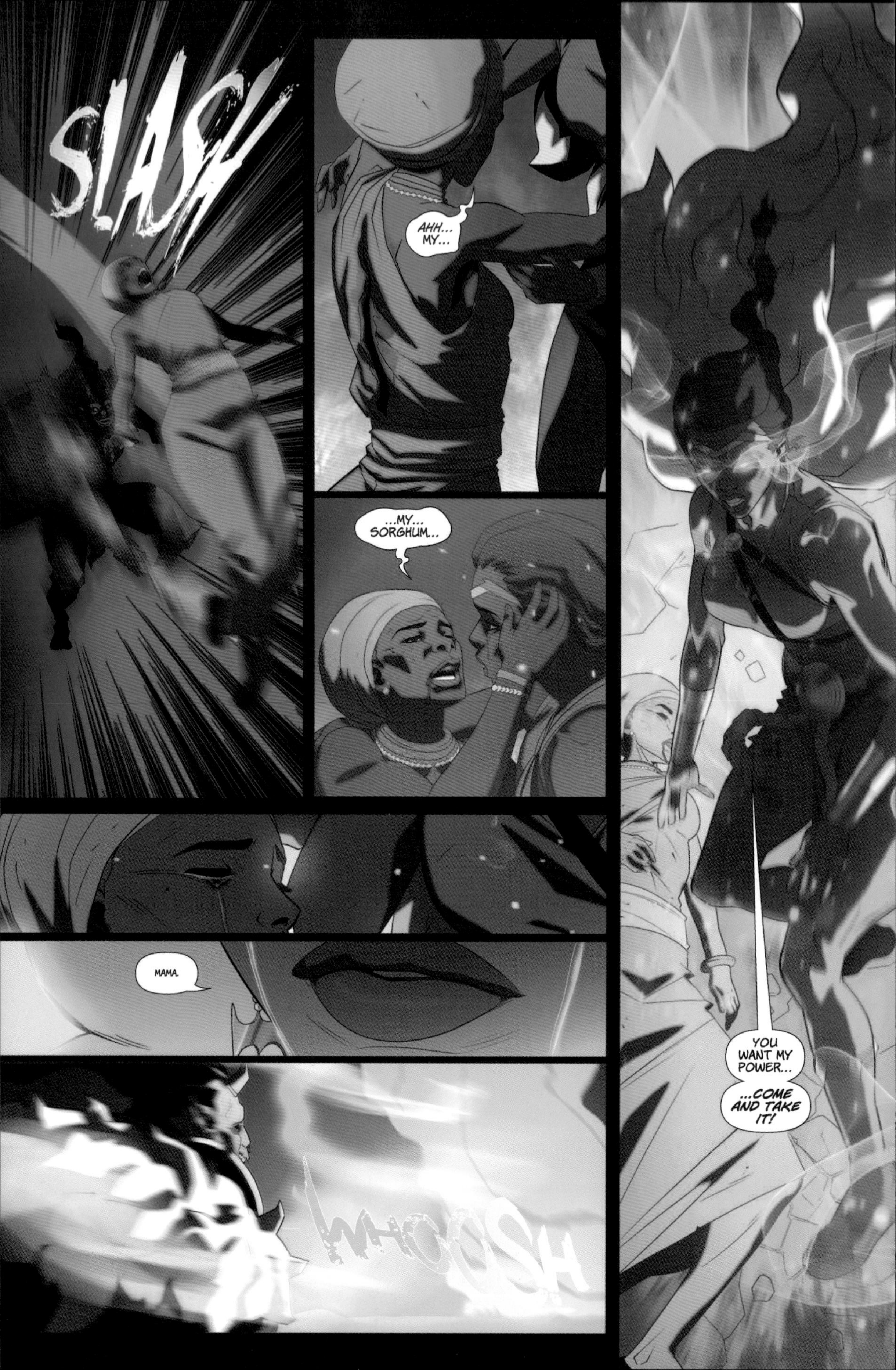
SLASH
AHH... MY...
...MY... SORGHUM...
MAMA.
YOU WANT MY POWER...
...COME AND TAKE IT!
WHOOSH

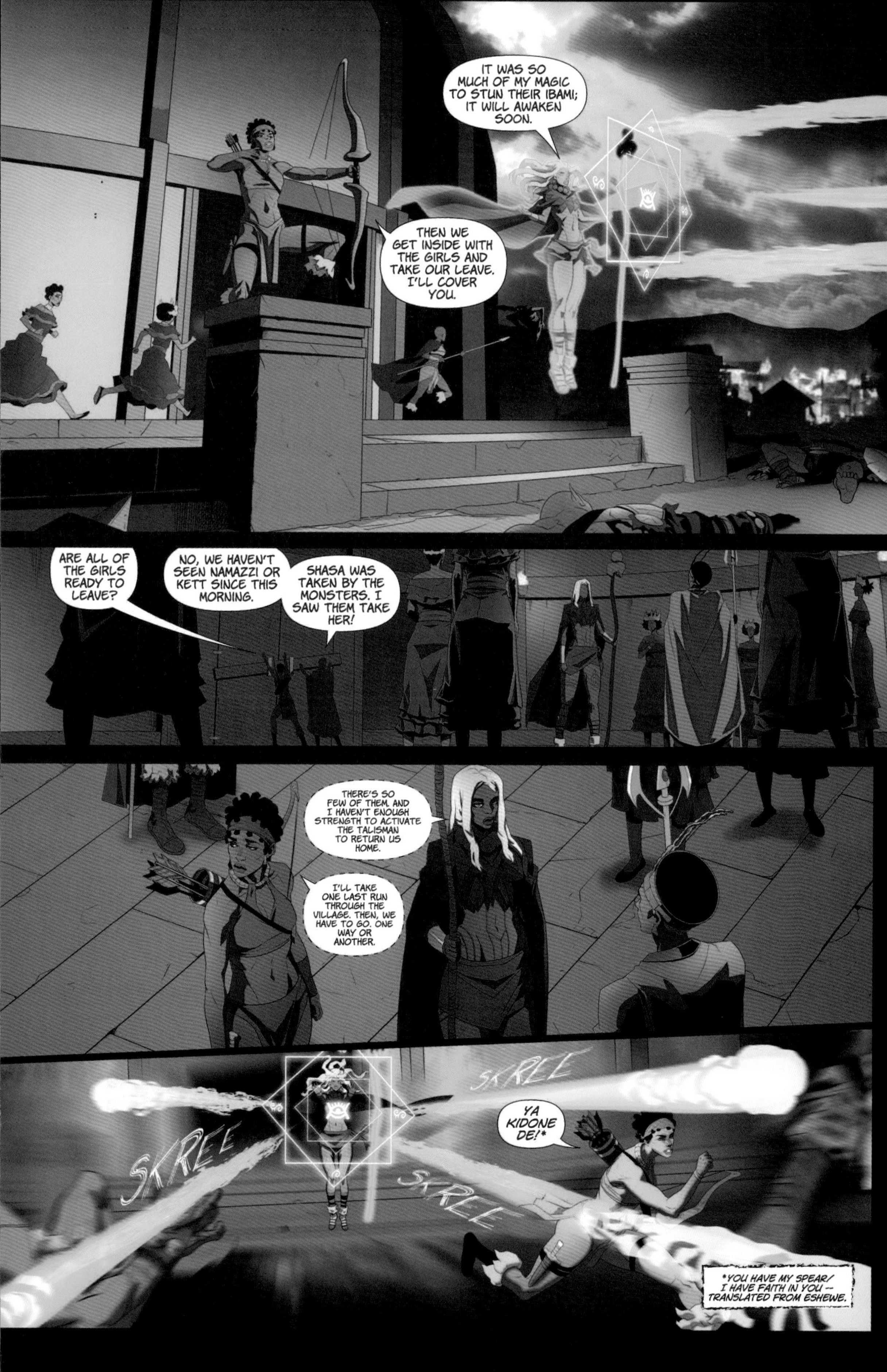
IT WAS SO MUCH OF MY MAGIC TO STUN THEIR IBAMI; IT WILL AWAKEN SOON.
THEN WE GET INSIDE WITH THE GIRLS AND TAKE OUR LEAVE. I'LL COVER YOU.
ARE ALL OF THE GIRLS READY TO LEAVE?
NO, WE HAVEN'T SEEN NAMAZZI OR KETT SINCE THIS MORNING.
SHASA WAS TAKEN BY THE MONSTERS. I SAW THEM TAKE HER!
THERE'S SO FEW OF THEM. AND I HAVEN'T ENOUGH STRENGTH TO ACTIVATE THE TALISMAN TO RETURN US HOME.
I'LL TAKE ONE LAST RUN THROUGH THE VILLAGE. THEN, WE HAVE TO GO. ONE WAY OR ANOTHER.
SKREE
SKREE
SKREE
YA KIDONE DE!*
*YOU HAVE MY SPEAR/ I HAVE FAITH IN YOU -- TRANSLATED FROM ESHEWE.

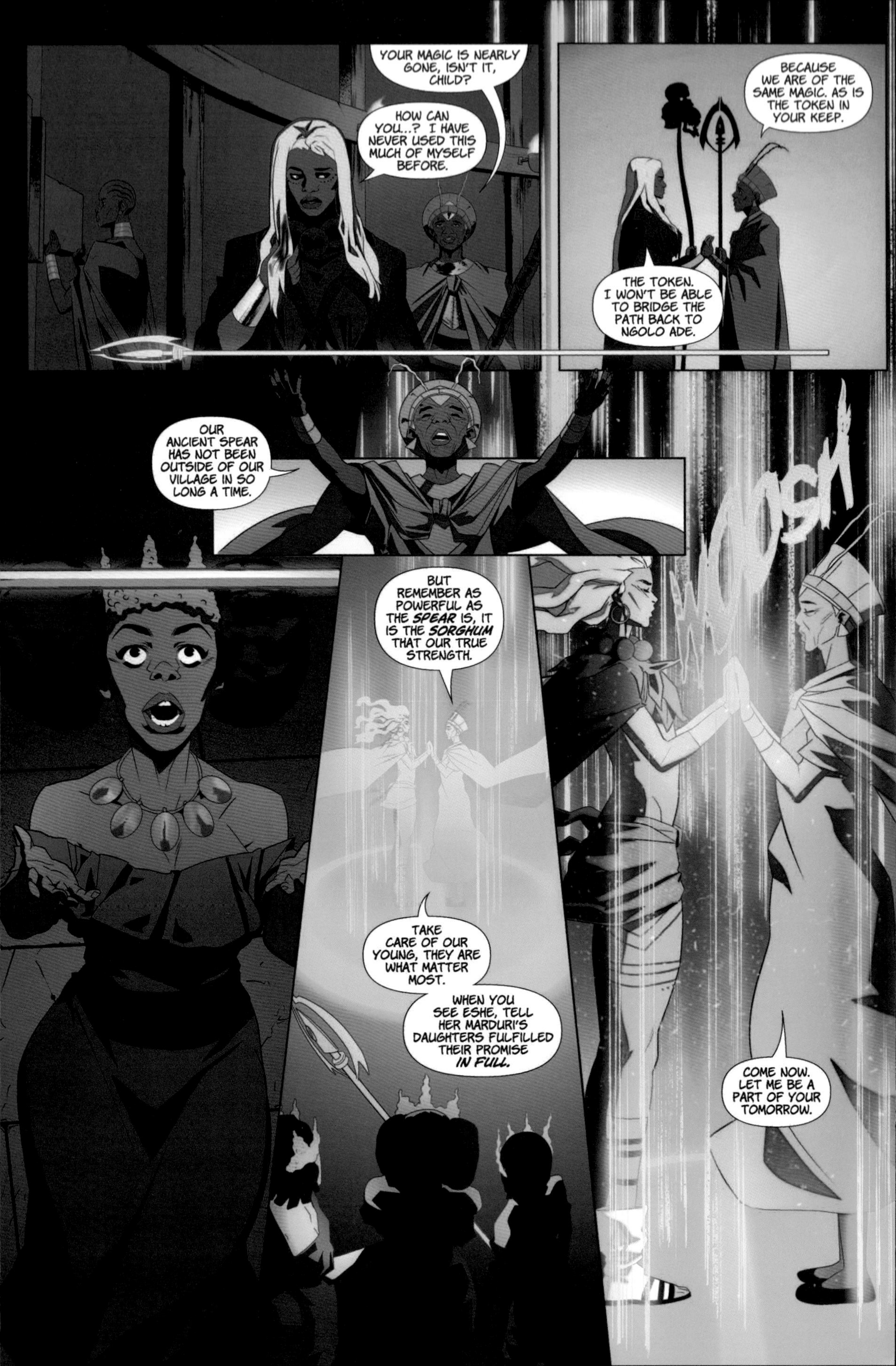
YOUR MAGIC IS NEARLY GONE, ISN'T IT, CHILD?
HOW CAN YOU...? I HAVE NEVER USED THIS MUCH OF MYSELF BEFORE.
BECAUSE WE ARE OF THE SAME MAGIC. AS IS THE TOKEN IN YOUR KEEP.
THE TOKEN. I WON'T BE ABLE TO BRIDGE THE PATH BACK TO NGOLO ADE.
OUR ANCIENT SPEAR HAS NOT BEEN OUTSIDE OF OUR VILLAGE IN SO LONG A TIME.
BUT REMEMBER AS POWERFUL AS THE SPEAR IS, IT IS THE SORGHUM THAT OUR TRUE STRENGTH.
TAKE CARE OF OUR YOUNG, THEY ARE WHAT MATTER MOST.
WHEN YOU SEE ESHE, TELL HER MARDURI'S DAUGHTERS FULFILLED THEIR PROMISE IN FULL.
WOOOSH
COME NOW. LET ME BE A PART OF YOUR TOMORROW.

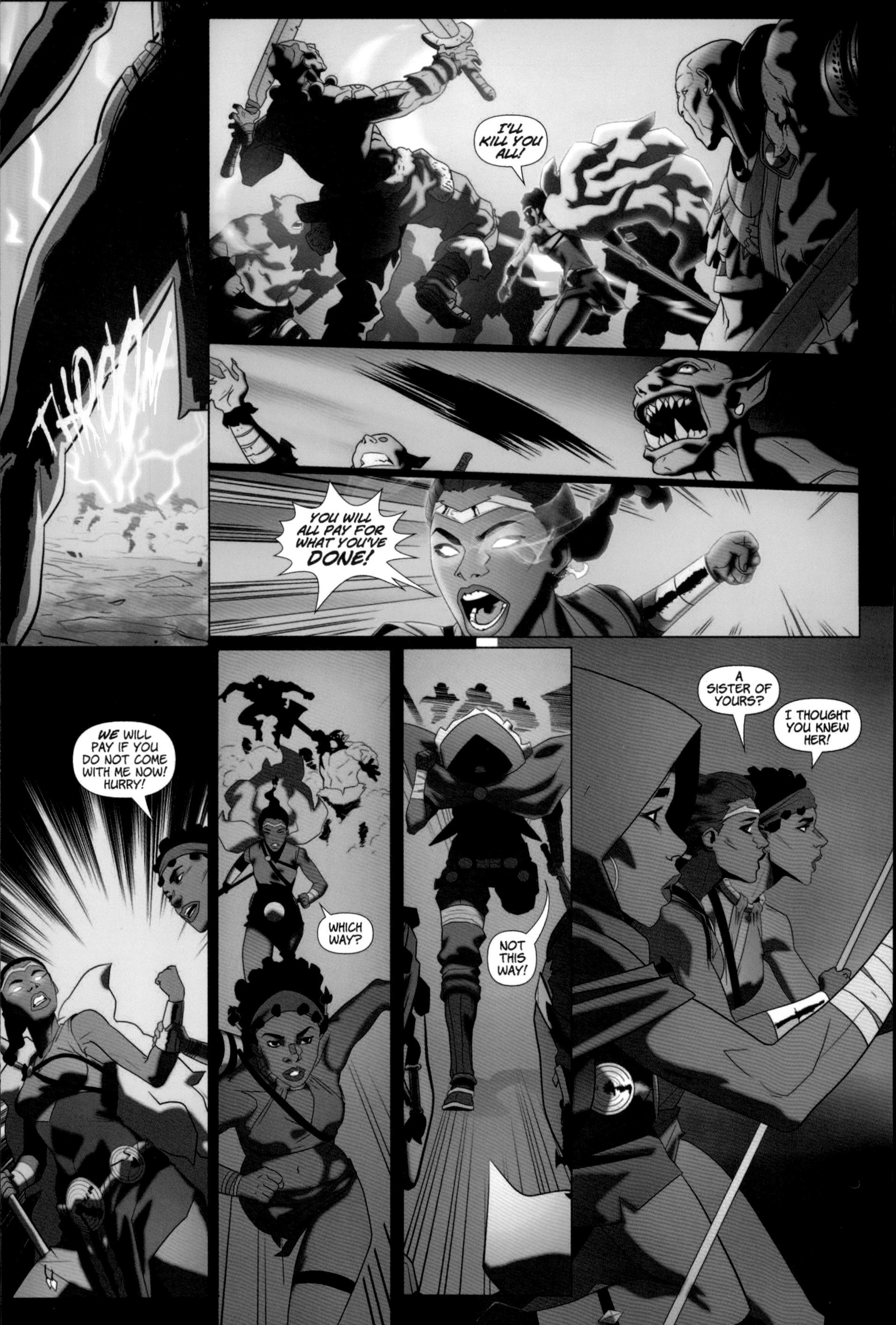
THROOM
I'LL KILL YOU ALL!
YOU WILL ALL PAY FOR WHAT YOU'VE DONE!
WE WILL PAY IF YOU DO NOT COME WITH ME NOW! HURRY!
WHICH WAY?
NOT THIS WAY!
A SISTER OF YOURS?
I THOUGHT YOU KNEW HER!

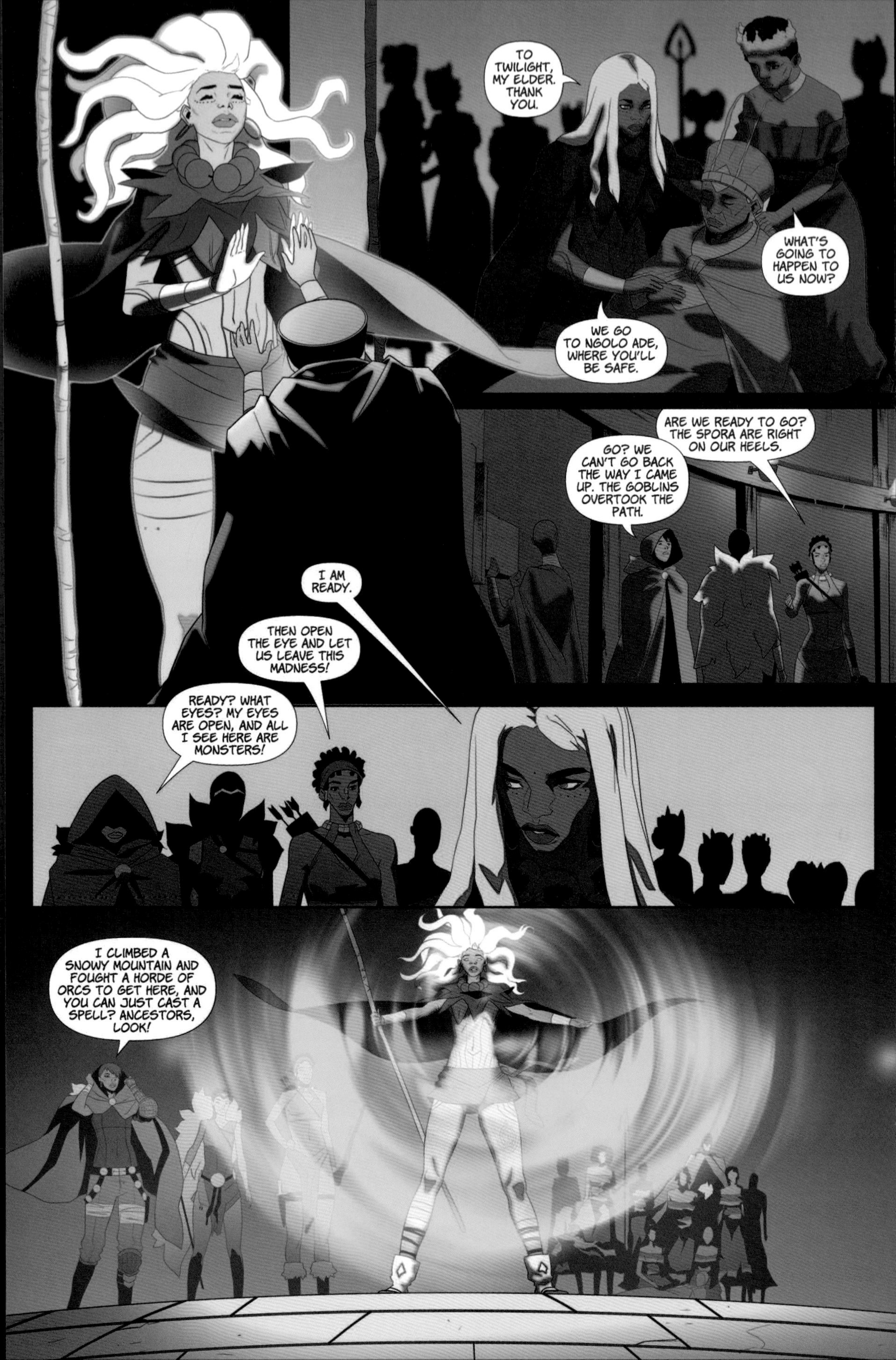
TO TWILIGHT, MY ELDER. THANK YOU.
WHAT'S GOING TO HAPPEN TO US NOW?
WE GO TO NGOLO ADE, WHERE YOU'LL BE SAFE.
ARE WE READY TO GO? THE SPORA ARE RIGHT ON OUR HEELS.
GO? WE CAN'T GO BACK THE WAY I CAME UP. THE GOBLINS OVERTOOK THE PATH.
I AM READY.
THEN OPEN THE EYE AND LET US LEAVE THIS MADNESS!
READY? WHAT EYES? MY EYES ARE OPEN, AND ALL I SEE HERE ARE MONSTERS!
I CLIMBED A SNOWY MOUNTAIN AND FOUGHT A HORDE OF ORCS TO GET HERE, AND YOU CAN JUST CAST A SPELL? ANCESTORS, LOOK!

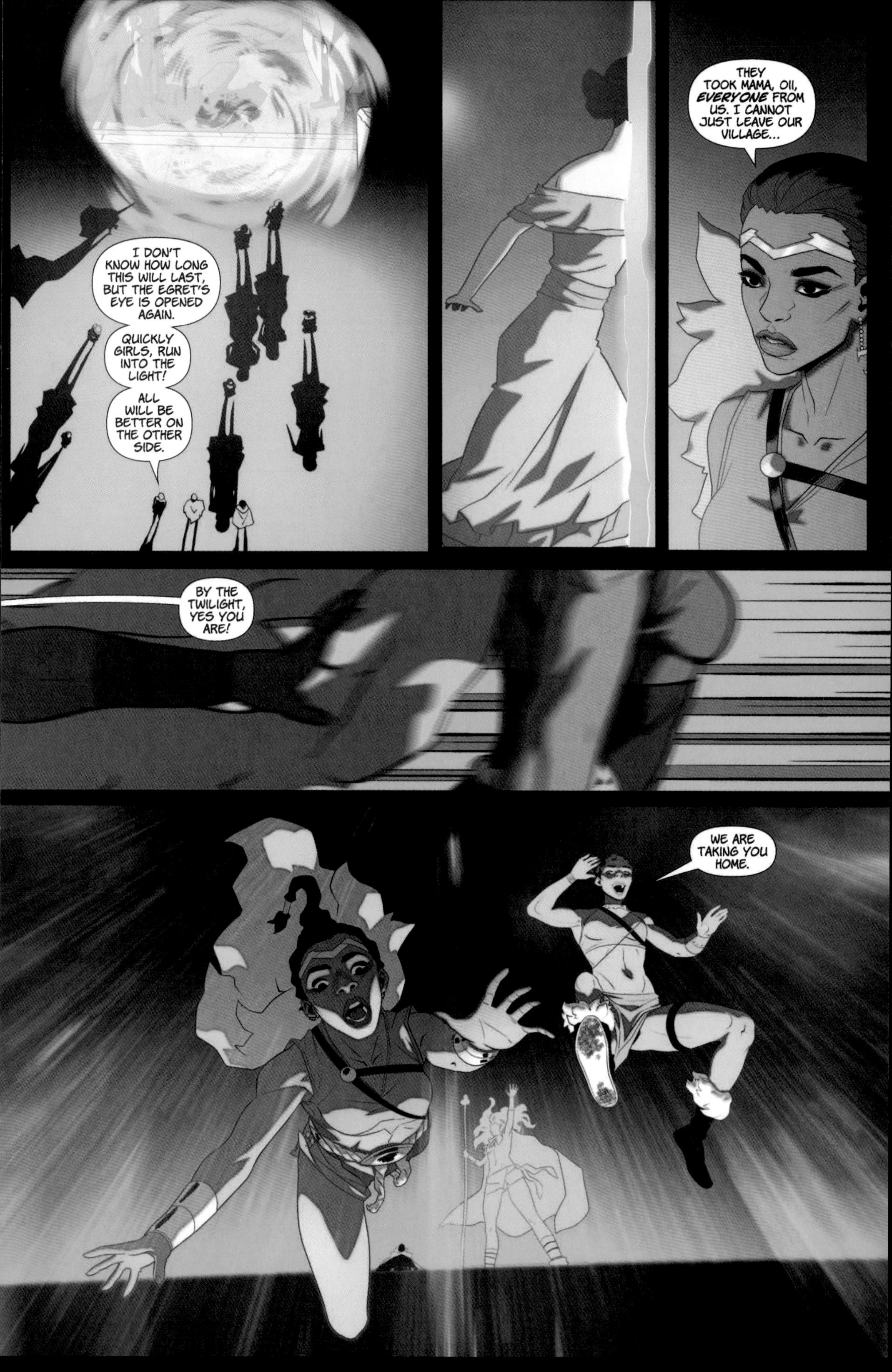
I DON'T KNOW HOW LONG THIS WILL LAST, BUT THE EGRET'S EYE IS OPENED AGAIN.
QUICKLY GIRLS, RUN INTO THE LIGHT!
ALL WILL BE BETTER ON THE OTHER SIDE.
THEY TOOK MAMA, OII, EVERYONE FROM US. I CANNOT JUST LEAVE OUR VILLAGE...
BY THE TWILIGHT, YES YOU ARE!
WE ARE TAKING YOU HOME.

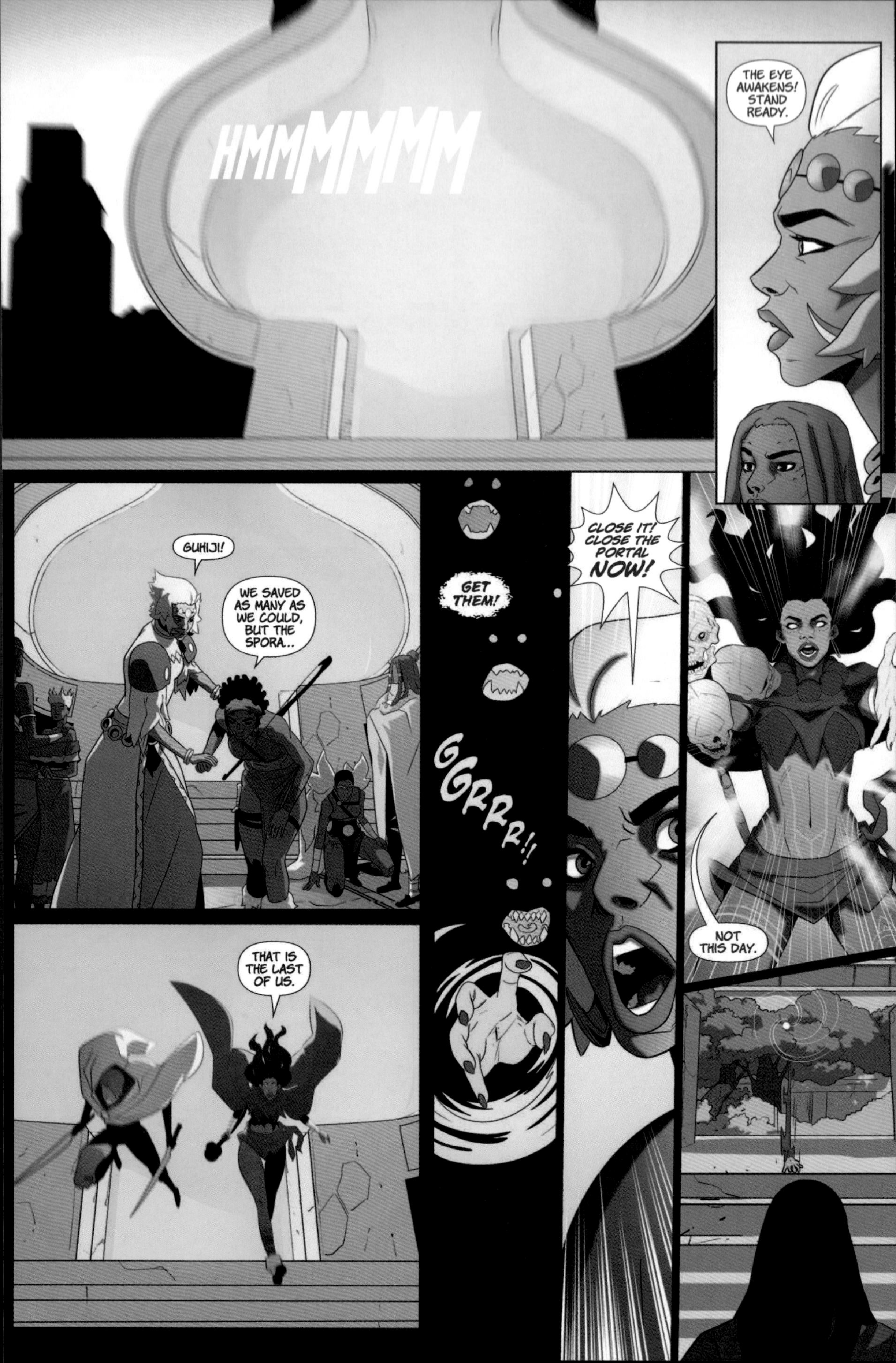
HMMMMMM
THE EYE AWAKENS! STAND READY.
GUHIJI!
WE SAVED AS MANY AS WE COULD, BUT THE SPORA...
THAT IS THE LAST OF US.
GET THEM!
GGRRR!!
CLOSE IT! CLOSE THE PORTAL NOW!
NOT THIS DAY.

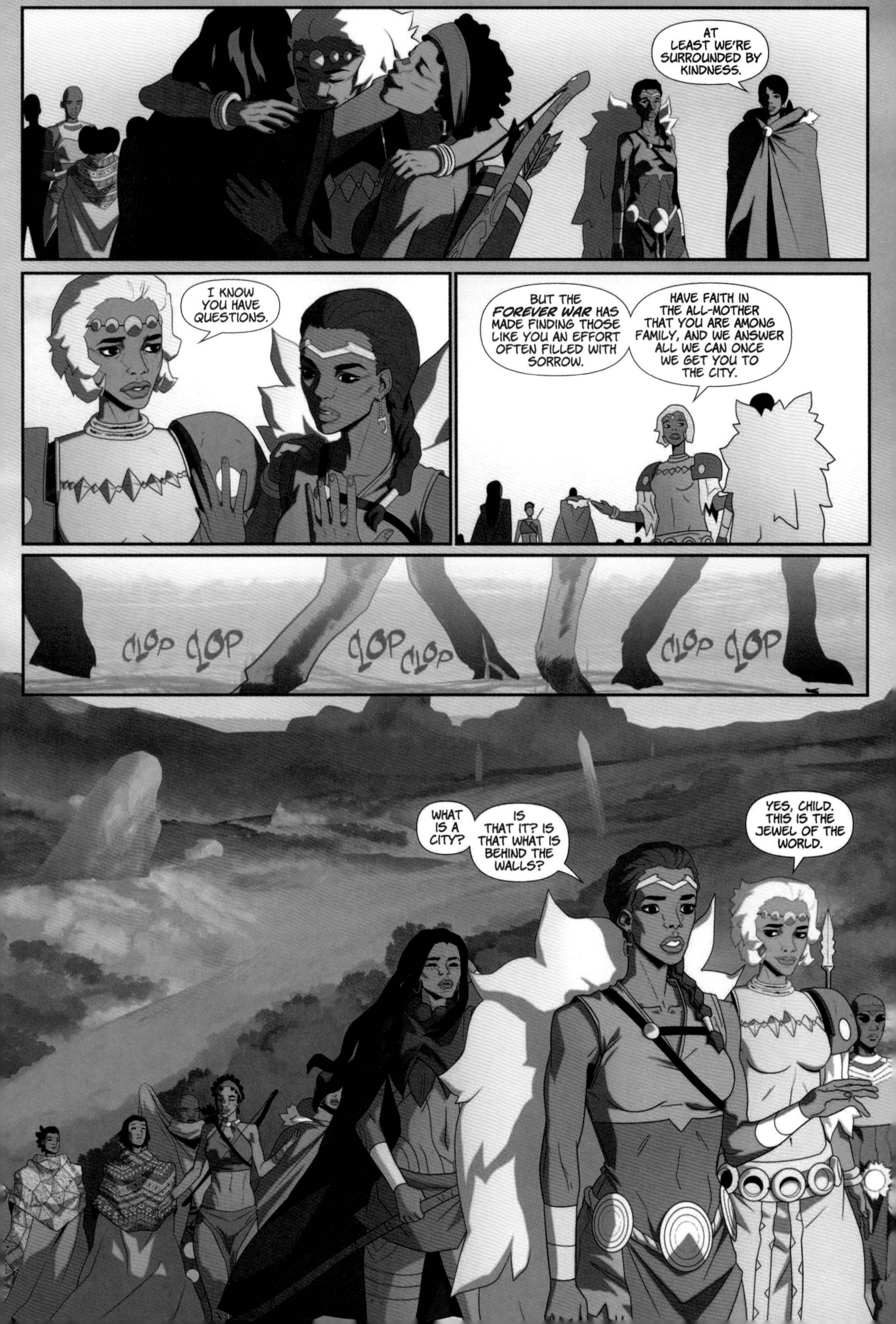
AT LEAST WE'RE SURROUNDED BY KINDNESS.
I KNOW YOU HAVE QUESTIONS.
BUT THE FOREVER WAR HAS MADE FINDING THOSE LIKE YOU AN EFFORT OFTEN FILLED WITH SORROW.
HAVE FAITH IN THE ALL-MOTHER THAT YOU ARE AMONG FAMILY, AND WE ANSWER ALL WE CAN ONCE WE GET YOU TO THE CITY.
CLOP CLOP
CLOP CLOP
CLOP CLOP
WHAT IS A CITY?
IS THAT IT? IS THAT WHAT IS BEHIND THE WALLS?
YES, CHILD. THIS IS THE JEWEL OF THE WORLD.

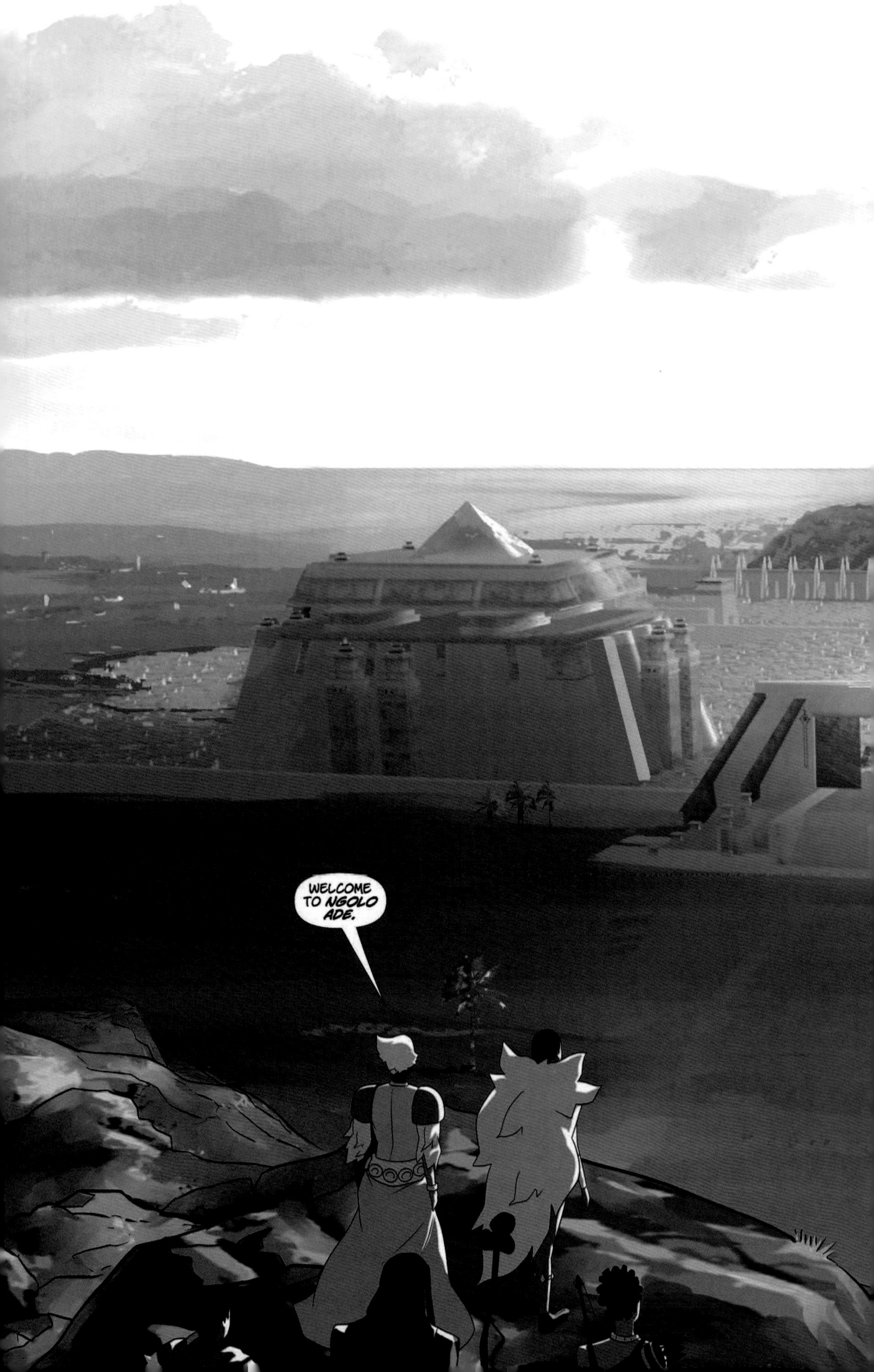
WELCOME TO NGOLO ADE.

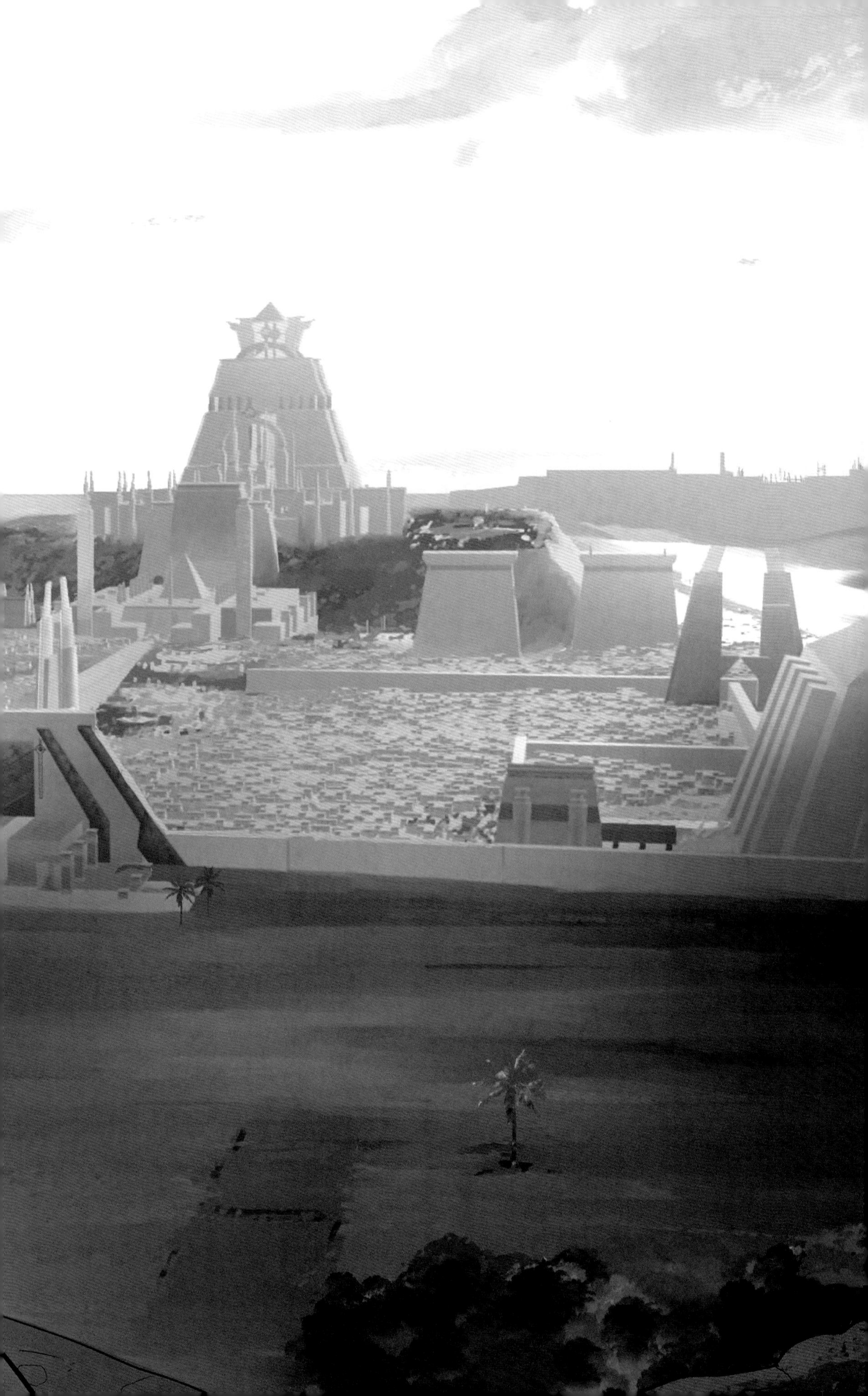

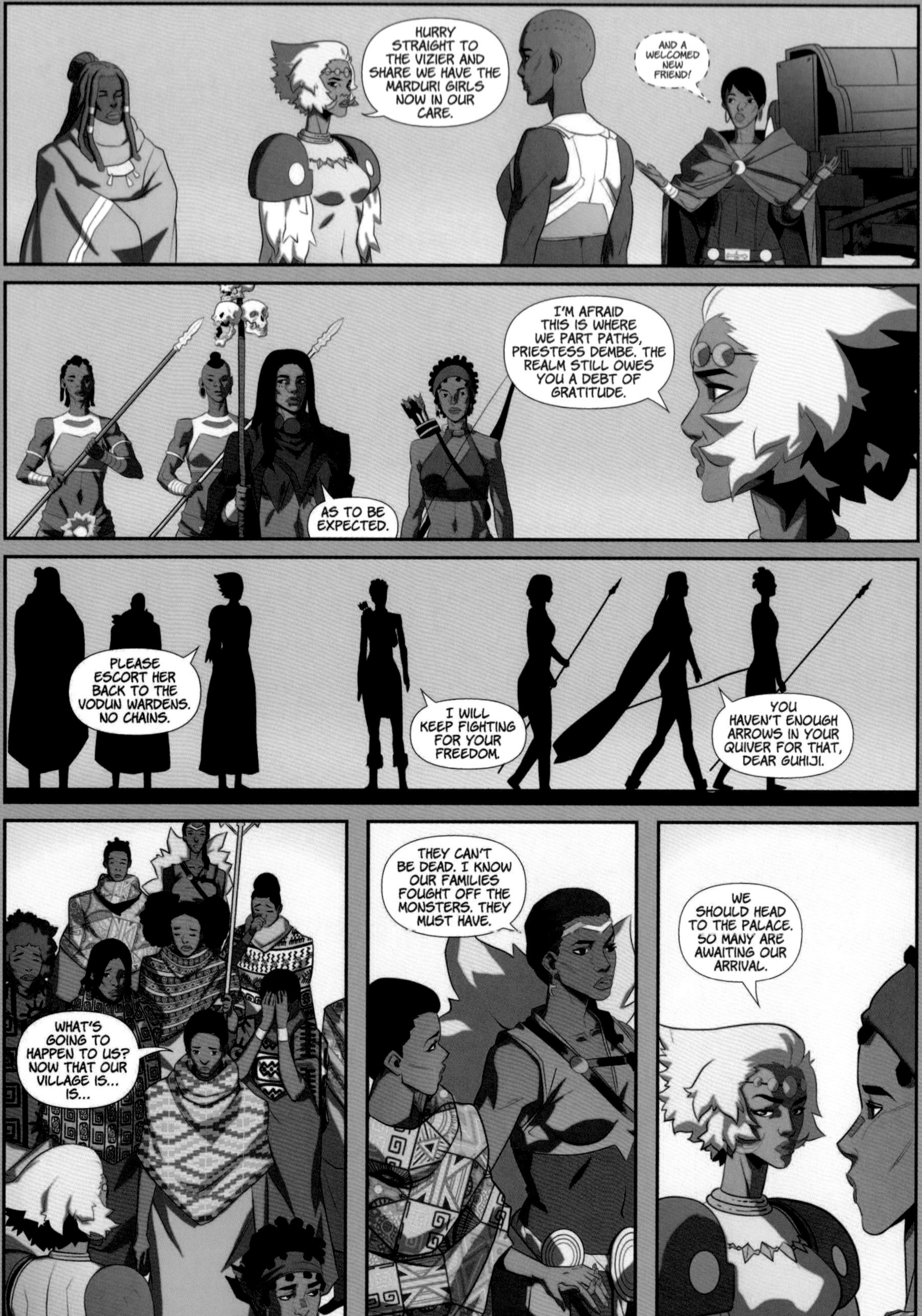
HURRY STRAIGHT TO THE VIZIER AND SHARE WE HAVE THE MARDURI GIRLS NOW IN OUR CARE.
AND A WELCOMED NEW FRIEND!
I'M AFRAID THIS IS WHERE WE PART PATHS, PRIESTESS DEMBE. THE REALM STILL OWES YOU A DEBT OF GRATITUDE.
AS TO BE EXPECTED.
PLEASE ESCORT HER BACK TO THE VODUN WARDENS. NO CHAINS.
I WILL KEEP FIGHTING FOR YOUR FREEDOM.
YOU HAVEN'T ENOUGH ARROWS IN YOUR QUIVER FOR THAT, DEAR GUHIJI.
WHAT'S GOING TO HAPPEN TO US? NOW THAT OUR VILLAGE IS... IS...
THEY CAN'T BE DEAD. I KNOW OUR FAMILIES FOUGHT OFF THE MONSTERS. THEY MUST HAVE.
WE SHOULD HEAD TO THE PALACE. SO MANY ARE AWAITING OUR ARRIVAL.

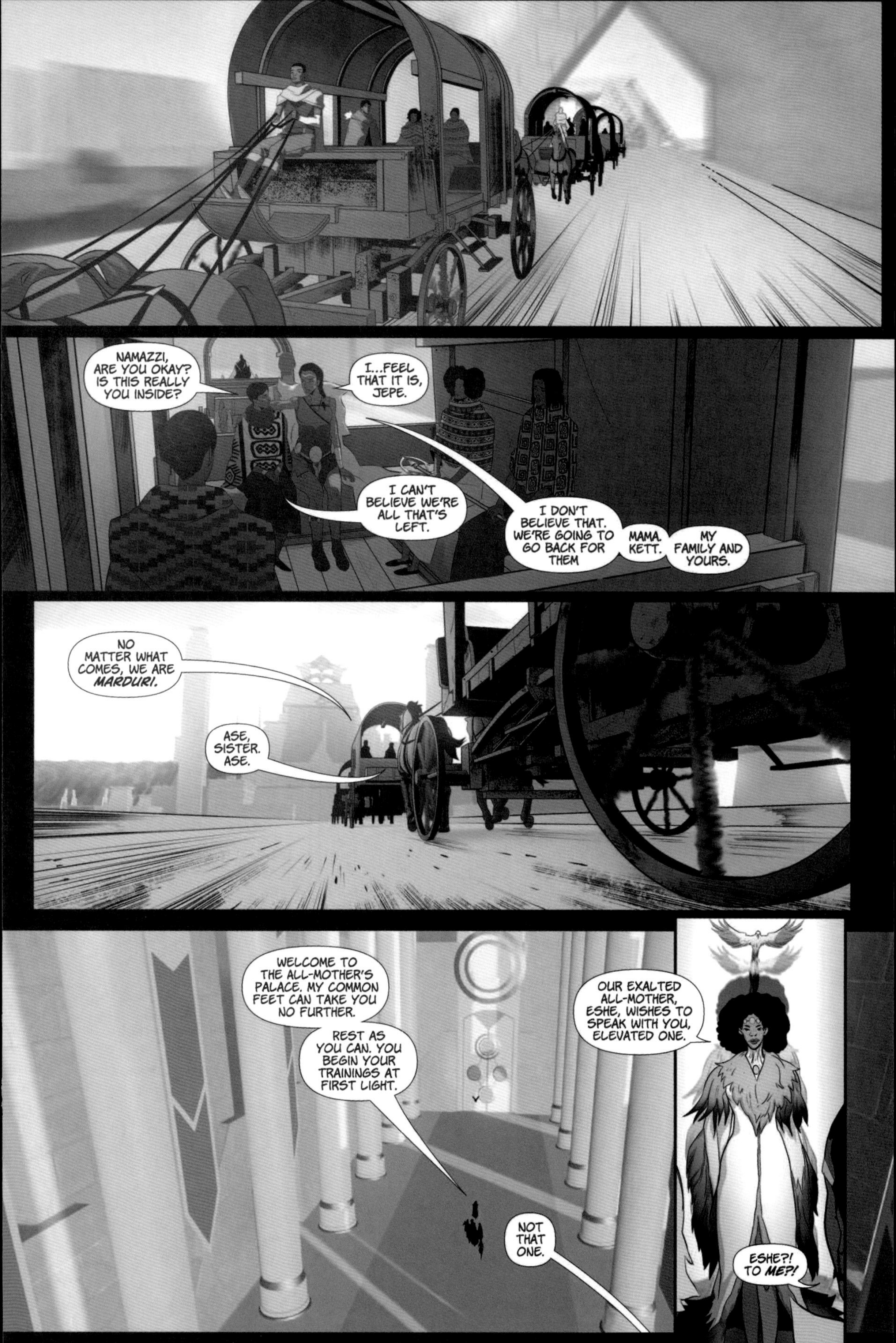
NAMAZZI, ARE YOU OKAY? IS THIS REALLY YOU INSIDE?
I...FEEL THAT IT IS, JEPE.
I CAN'T BELIEVE WE'RE ALL THAT'S LEFT.
I DON'T BELIEVE THAT. WE'RE GOING TO GO BACK FOR THEM
MAMA. KETT.
MY FAMILY AND YOURS.
NO MATTER WHAT COMES, WE ARE *MARDURI.*
ASE, SISTER. ASE.
WELCOME TO THE ALL-MOTHER'S PALACE. MY COMMON FEET CAN TAKE YOU NO FURTHER.
REST AS YOU CAN. YOU BEGIN YOUR TRAININGS AT FIRST LIGHT.
NOT THAT ONE.
OUR EXALTED ALL-MOTHER, ESHE, WISHES TO SPEAK WITH YOU, ELEVATED ONE.
ESHE?! TO *ME?!*

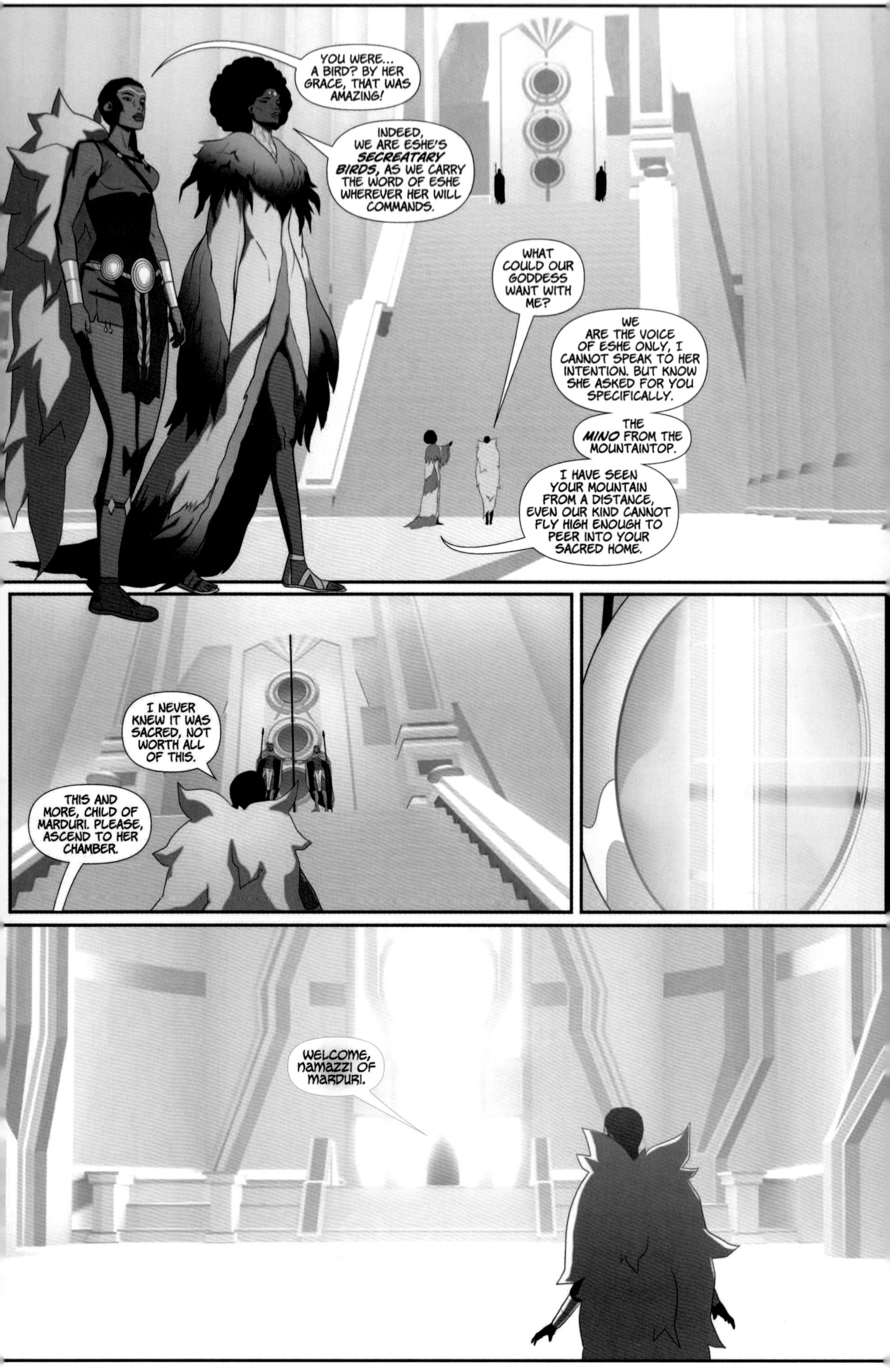
YOU WERE... A BIRD? BY HER GRACE, THAT WAS AMAZING!
INDEED, WE ARE ESHE'S ***SECREATARY BIRDS***, AS WE CARRY THE WORD OF ESHE WHEREVER HER WILL COMMANDS.
WHAT COULD OUR GODDESS WANT WITH ME?
WE ARE THE VOICE OF ESHE ONLY, I CANNOT SPEAK TO HER INTENTION. BUT KNOW SHE ASKED FOR YOU SPECIFICALLY.
THE ***MINO*** FROM THE MOUNTAINTOP.
I HAVE SEEN YOUR MOUNTAIN FROM A DISTANCE, EVEN OUR KIND CANNOT FLY HIGH ENOUGH TO PEER INTO YOUR SACRED HOME.
I NEVER KNEW IT WAS SACRED, NOT WORTH ALL OF THIS.
THIS AND MORE, CHILD OF MARDURI. PLEASE, ASCEND TO HER CHAMBER.
WELCOME, NAMAZZI OF MARDURI.

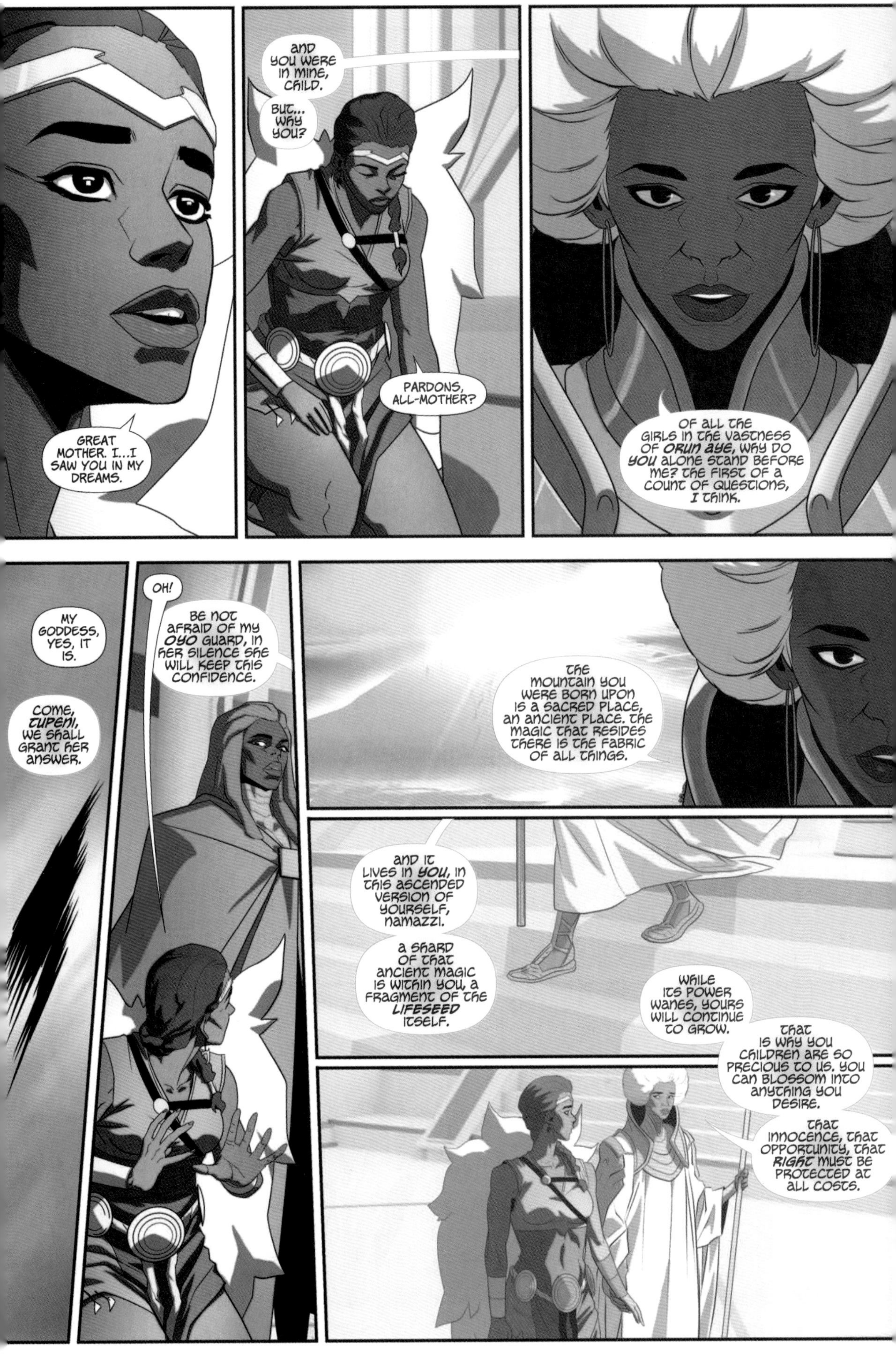
GREAT MOTHER. I...I SAW YOU IN MY DREAMS.
AND YOU WERE IN MINE, CHILD.
BUT... WHY YOU?
PARDONS, ALL-MOTHER?
OF ALL THE GIRLS IN THE VASTNESS OF ORUN AYE, WHY DO YOU ALONE STAND BEFORE ME? THE FIRST OF A COUNT OF QUESTIONS, I THINK.
MY GODDESS, YES, IT IS.
COME, TUPENI, WE SHALL GRANT HER ANSWER.
OH!
BE NOT AFRAID OF MY OYO GUARD, IN HER SILENCE SHE WILL KEEP THIS CONFIDENCE.
THE MOUNTAIN YOU WERE BORN UPON IS A SACRED PLACE, AN ANCIENT PLACE. THE MAGIC THAT RESIDES THERE IS THE FABRIC OF ALL THINGS.
AND IT LIVES IN YOU, IN THIS ASCENDED VERSION OF YOURSELF, NAMAZZI.
A SHARD OF THAT ANCIENT MAGIC IS WITHIN YOU, A FRAGMENT OF THE LIFESEED ITSELF.
WHILE ITS POWER WANES, YOURS WILL CONTINUE TO GROW.
THAT IS WHY YOU CHILDREN ARE SO PRECIOUS TO US. YOU CAN BLOSSOM INTO ANYTHING YOU DESIRE.
THAT INNOCENCE, THAT OPPORTUNITY, THAT RIGHT MUST BE PROTECTED AT ALL COSTS.

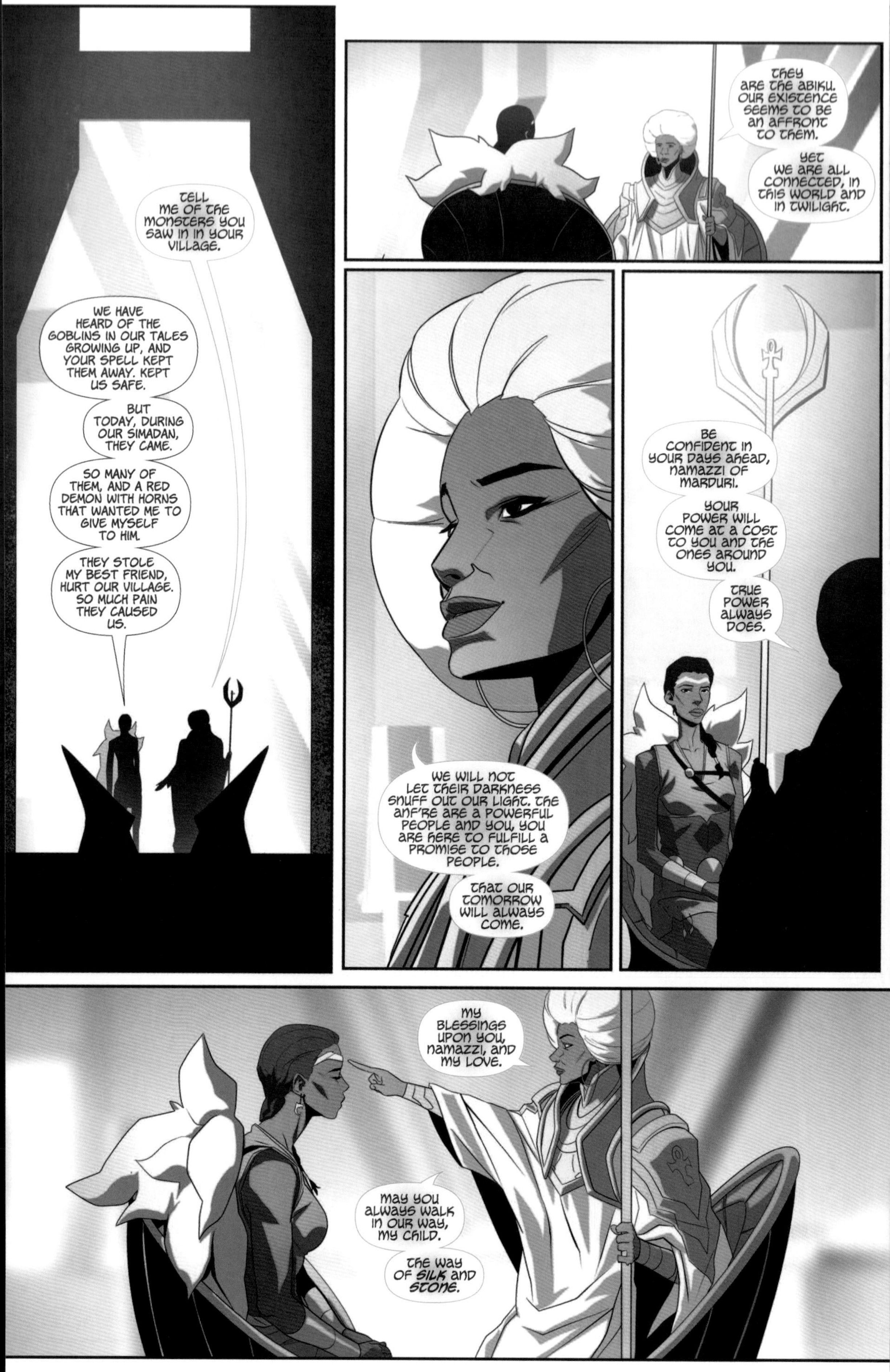
TELL ME OF THE MONSTERS YOU SAW IN IN YOUR VILLAGE.
WE HAVE HEARD OF THE GOBLINS IN OUR TALES GROWING UP, AND YOUR SPELL KEPT THEM AWAY. KEPT US SAFE.
BUT TODAY, DURING OUR SIMADAN, THEY CAME.
SO MANY OF THEM, AND A RED DEMON WITH HORNS THAT WANTED ME TO GIVE MYSELF TO HIM.
THEY STOLE MY BEST FRIEND, HURT OUR VILLAGE. SO MUCH PAIN THEY CAUSED US.
THEY ARE THE ABIKU. OUR EXISTENCE SEEMS TO BE AN AFFRONT TO THEM.
YET WE ARE ALL CONNECTED, IN THIS WORLD AND IN TWILIGHT.
WE WILL NOT LET THEIR DARKNESS SNUFF OUT OUR LIGHT. THE ANF'RE ARE A POWERFUL PEOPLE AND YOU, YOU ARE HERE TO FULFILL A PROMISE TO THOSE PEOPLE.
THAT OUR TOMORROW WILL ALWAYS COME.
BE CONFIDENT IN YOUR DAYS AHEAD, NAMAZZI OF MARDURI.
YOUR POWER WILL COME AT A COST TO YOU AND THE ONES AROUND YOU.
TRUE POWER ALWAYS DOES.
MY BLESSINGS UPON YOU, NAMAZZI, AND MY LOVE.
MAY YOU ALWAYS WALK IN OUR WAY, MY CHILD.
THE WAY OF SILK AND STONE.

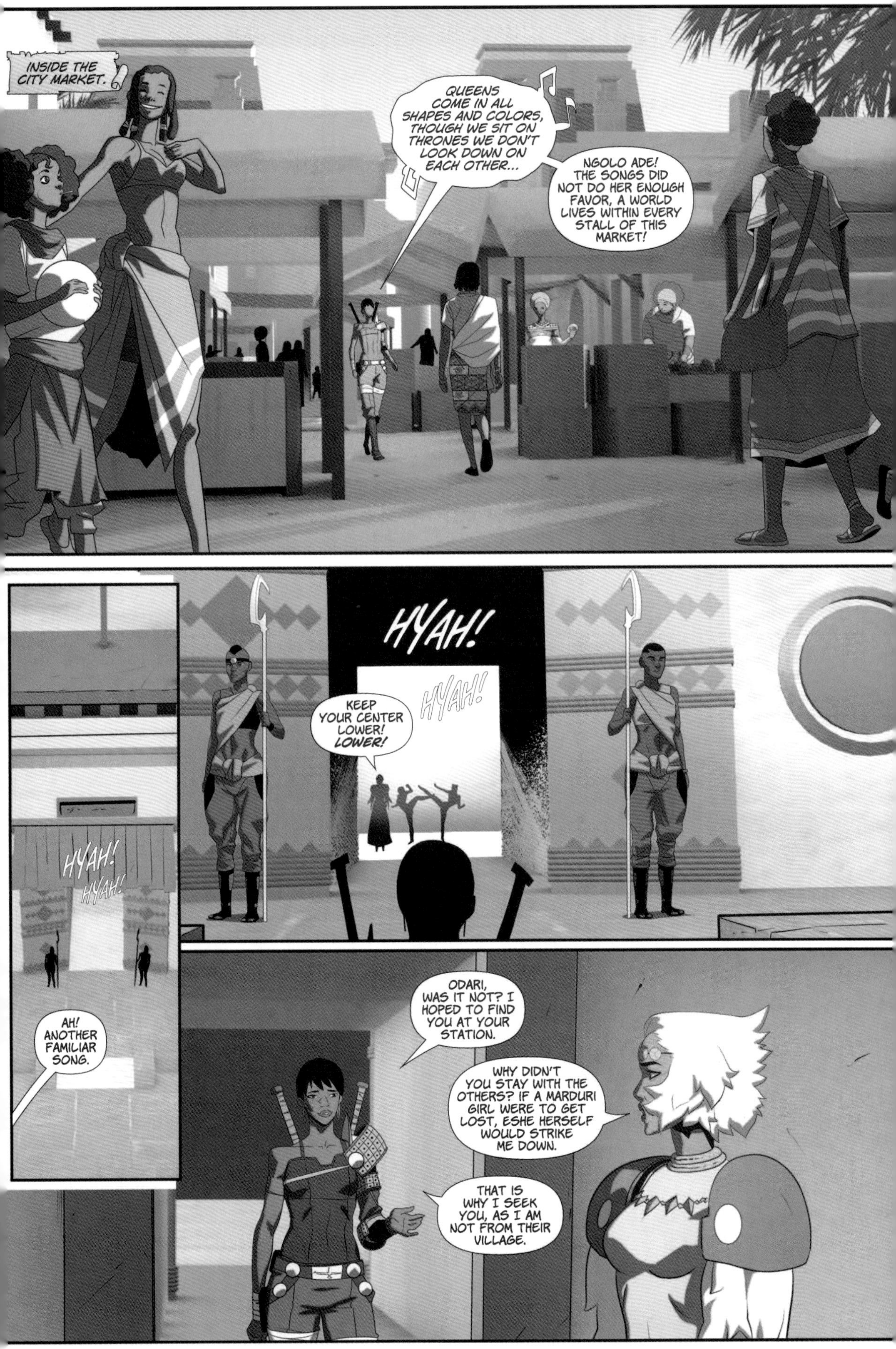
INSIDE THE CITY MARKET.
QUEENS COME IN ALL SHAPES AND COLORS, THOUGH WE SIT ON THRONES WE DON'T LOOK DOWN ON EACH OTHER...
NGOLO ADE! THE SONGS DID NOT DO HER ENOUGH FAVOR, A WORLD LIVES WITHIN EVERY STALL OF THIS MARKET!
HYAH! HYAH!
AH! ANOTHER FAMILIAR SONG.
HYAH!
HYAH!
KEEP YOUR CENTER LOWER! LOWER!
ODARI, WAS IT NOT? I HOPED TO FIND YOU AT YOUR STATION.
WHY DIDN'T YOU STAY WITH THE OTHERS? IF A MARDURI GIRL WERE TO GET LOST, ESHE HERSELF WOULD STRIKE ME DOWN.
THAT IS WHY I SEEK YOU, AS I AM NOT FROM THEIR VILLAGE.

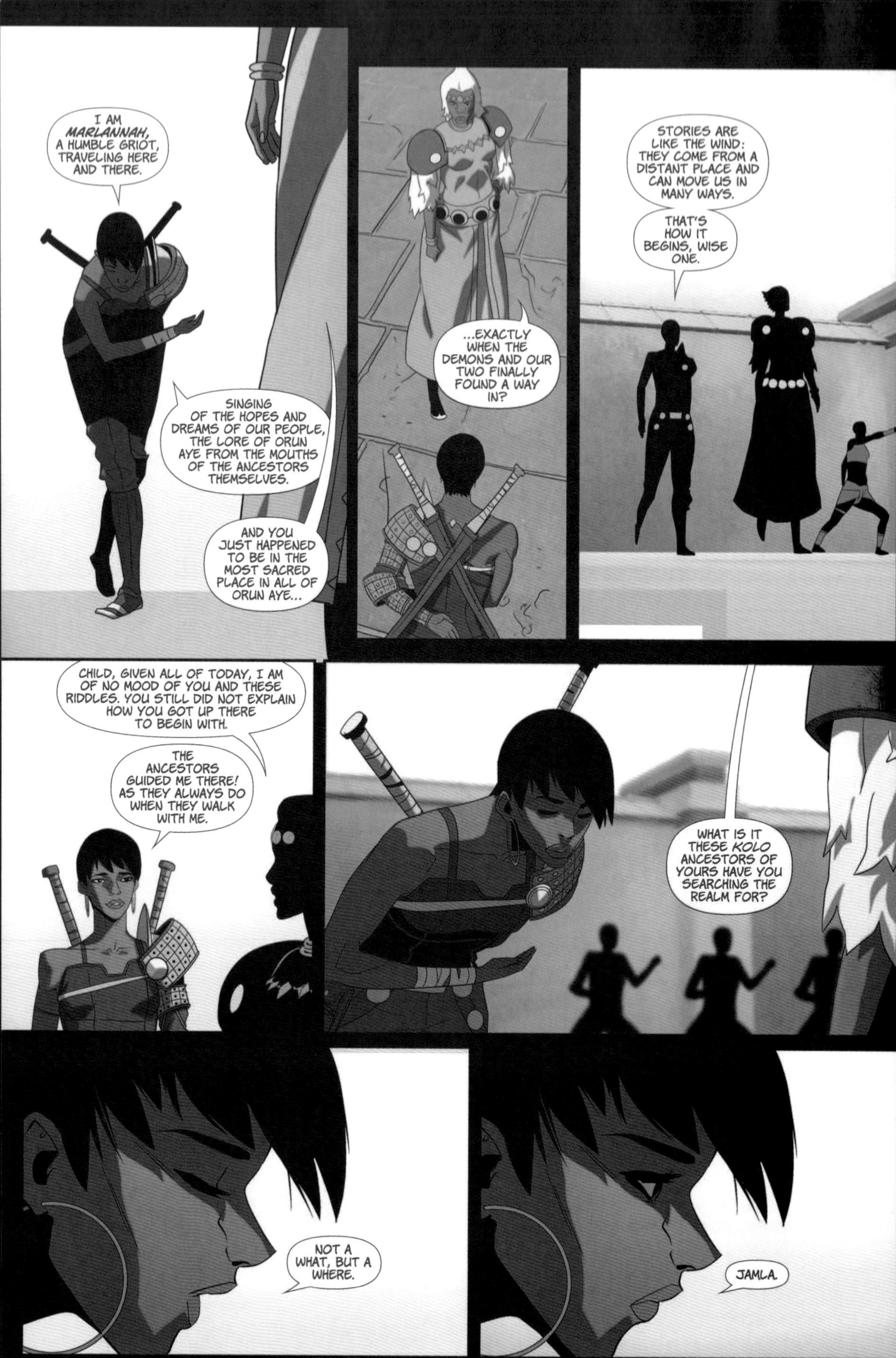
I AM *MARLANNAH*, A HUMBLE GRIOT, TRAVELING HERE AND THERE.
SINGING OF THE HOPES AND DREAMS OF OUR PEOPLE, THE LORE OF ORUN AYE FROM THE MOUTHS OF THE ANCESTORS THEMSELVES.
AND YOU JUST HAPPENED TO BE IN THE MOST SACRED PLACE IN ALL OF ORUN AYE...
...EXACTLY WHEN THE DEMONS AND OUR TWO FINALLY FOUND A WAY IN?
STORIES ARE LIKE THE WIND: THEY COME FROM A DISTANT PLACE AND CAN MOVE US IN MANY WAYS.
THAT'S HOW IT BEGINS, WISE ONE.
CHILD, GIVEN ALL OF TODAY, I AM OF NO MOOD OF YOU AND THESE RIDDLES. YOU STILL DID NOT EXPLAIN HOW YOU GOT UP THERE TO BEGIN WITH.
THE ANCESTORS GUIDED ME THERE! AS THEY ALWAYS DO WHEN THEY WALK WITH ME.
WHAT IS IT THESE *KOLO* ANCESTORS OF YOURS HAVE YOU SEARCHING THE REALM FOR?
NOT A WHAT, BUT A WHERE.
JAMLA.

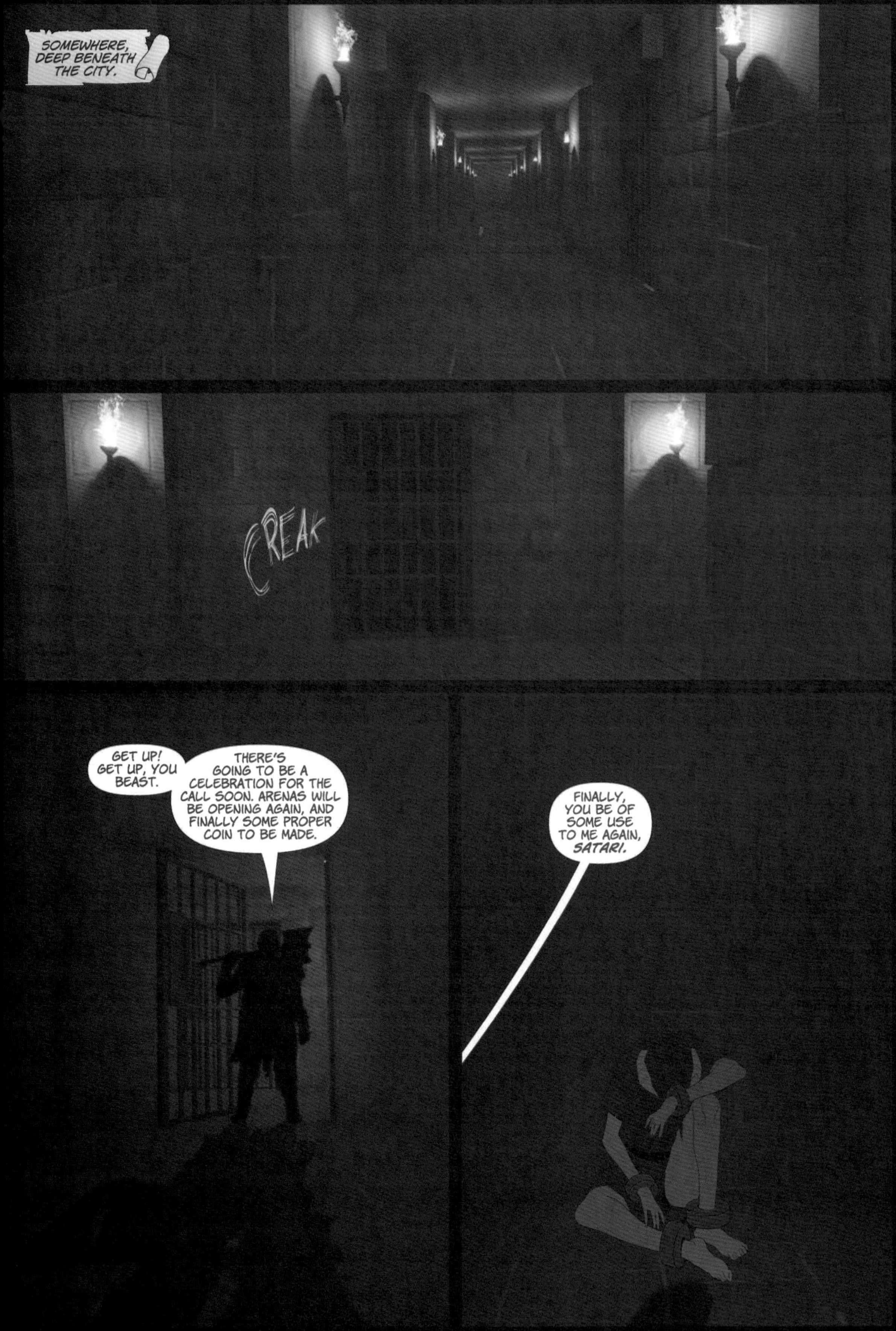
SOMEWHERE, DEEP BENEATH THE CITY.
CREAK
GET UP! GET UP, YOU BEAST.
THERE'S GOING TO BE A CELEBRATION FOR THE CALL SOON. ARENAS WILL BE OPENING AGAIN, AND FINALLY SOME PROPER COIN TO BE MADE.
FINALLY, YOU BE OF SOME USE TO ME AGAIN, SATARI.

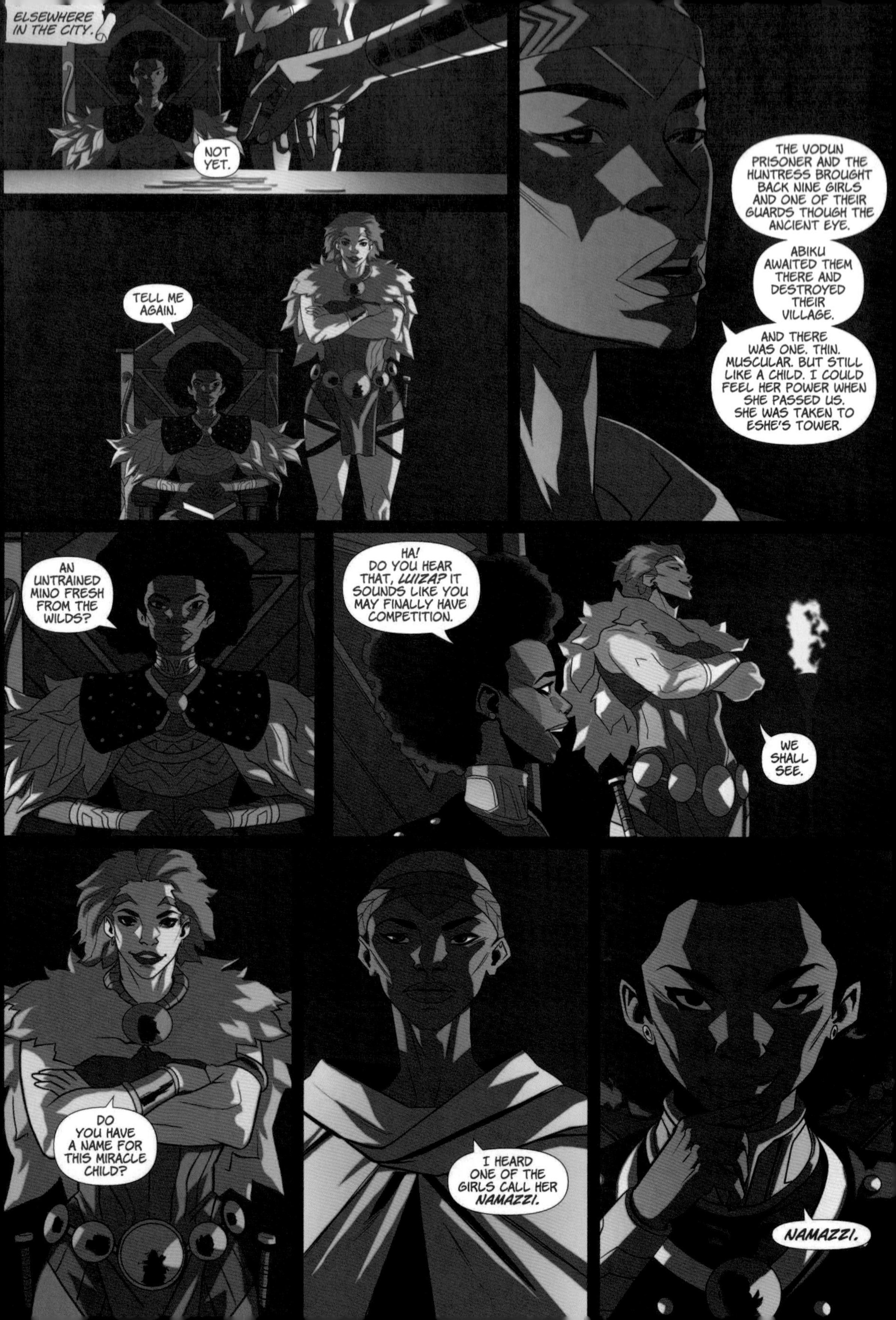
ELSEWHERE IN THE CITY.
NOT YET.
THE VODUN PRISONER AND THE HUNTRESS BROUGHT BACK NINE GIRLS AND ONE OF THEIR GUARDS THOUGH THE ANCIENT EYE.
ABIKU AWAITED THEM THERE AND DESTROYED THEIR VILLAGE.
AND THERE WAS ONE. THIN. MUSCULAR. BUT STILL LIKE A CHILD. I COULD FEEL HER POWER WHEN SHE PASSED US. SHE WAS TAKEN TO ESHE'S TOWER.
TELL ME AGAIN.
AN UNTRAINED MINO FRESH FROM THE WILDS?
HA! DO YOU HEAR THAT, LUIZA? IT SOUNDS LIKE YOU MAY FINALLY HAVE COMPETITION.
WE SHALL SEE.
DO YOU HAVE A NAME FOR THIS MIRACLE CHILD?
I HEARD ONE OF THE GIRLS CALL HER NAMAZZI.
NAMAZZI.

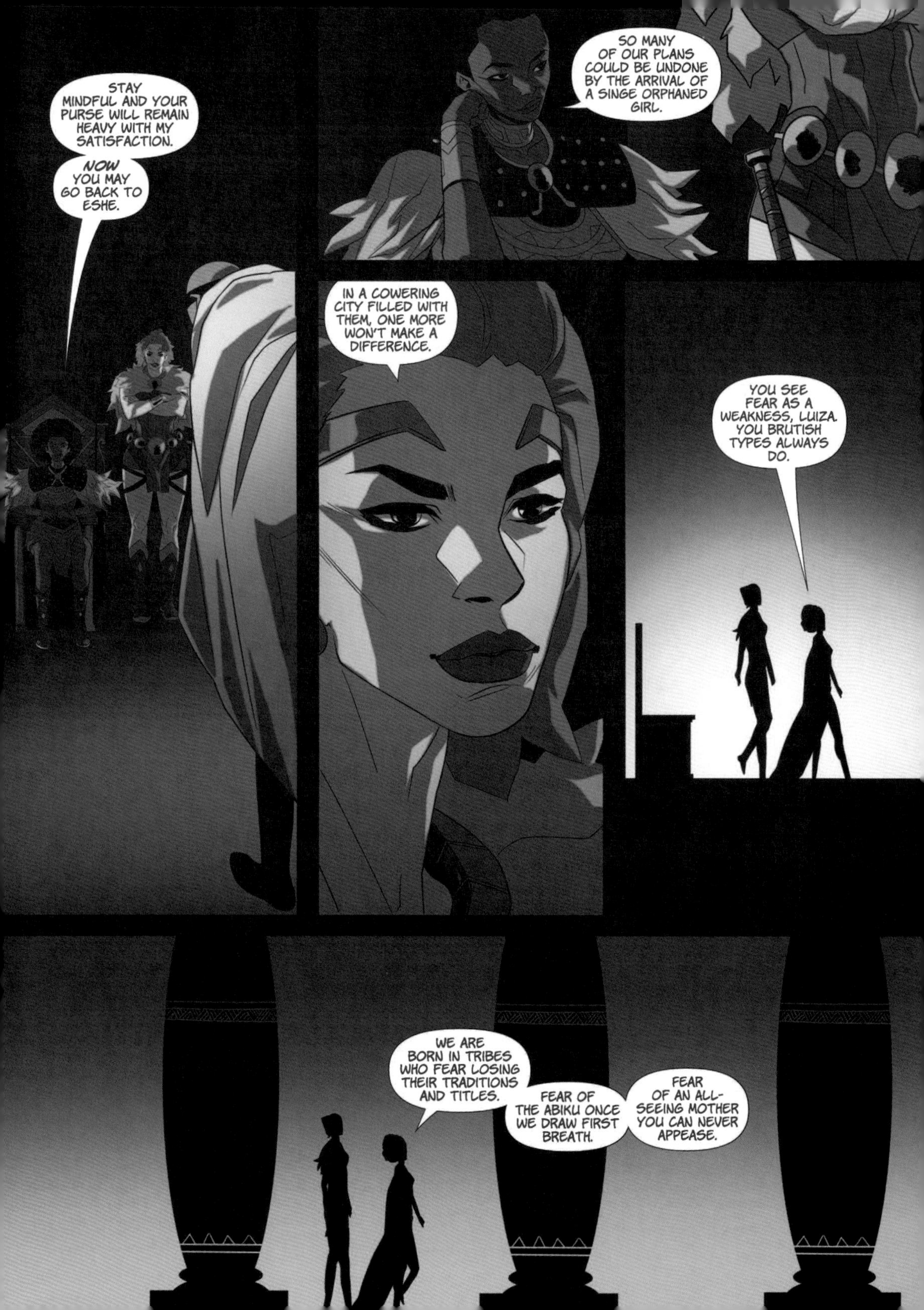
STAY MINDFUL AND YOUR PURSE WILL REMAIN HEAVY WITH MY SATISFACTION.
NOW YOU MAY GO BACK TO ESHE.
SO MANY OF OUR PLANS COULD BE UNDONE BY THE ARRIVAL OF A SINGE ORPHANED GIRL.
IN A COWERING CITY FILLED WITH THEM, ONE MORE WON'T MAKE A DIFFERENCE.
YOU SEE FEAR AS A WEAKNESS, LUIZA. YOU BRUTISH TYPES ALWAYS DO.
WE ARE BORN IN TRIBES WHO FEAR LOSING THEIR TRADITIONS AND TITLES.
FEAR OF THE ABIKU ONCE WE DRAW FIRST BREATH.
FEAR OF AN ALL-SEEING MOTHER YOU CAN NEVER APPEASE.

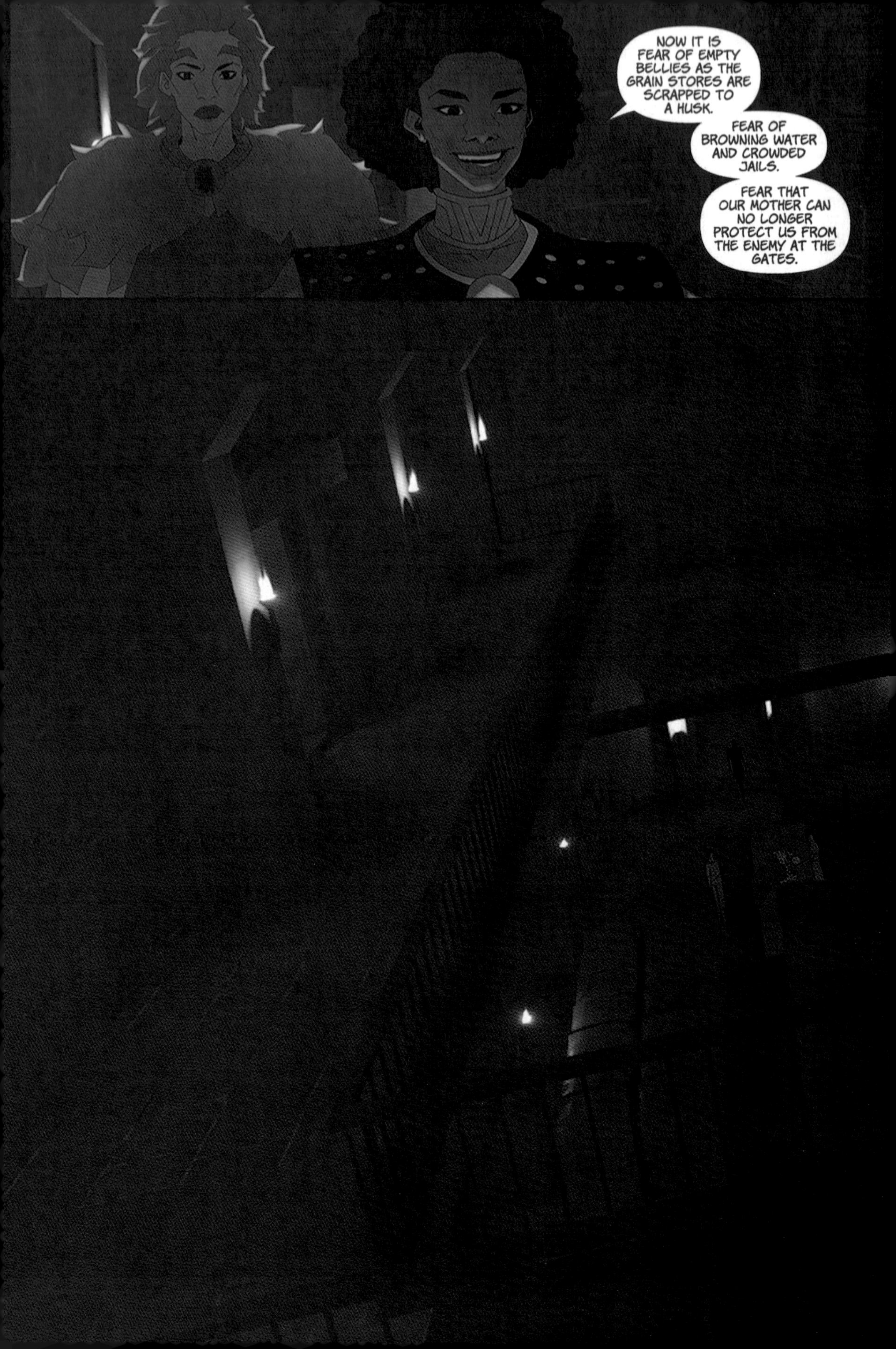
NOW IT IS FEAR OF EMPTY BELLIES AS THE GRAIN STORES ARE SCRAPPED TO A HUSK.
FEAR OF BROWNING WATER AND CROWDED JAILS.
FEAR THAT OUR MOTHER CAN NO LONGER PROTECT US FROM THE ENEMY AT THE GATES.

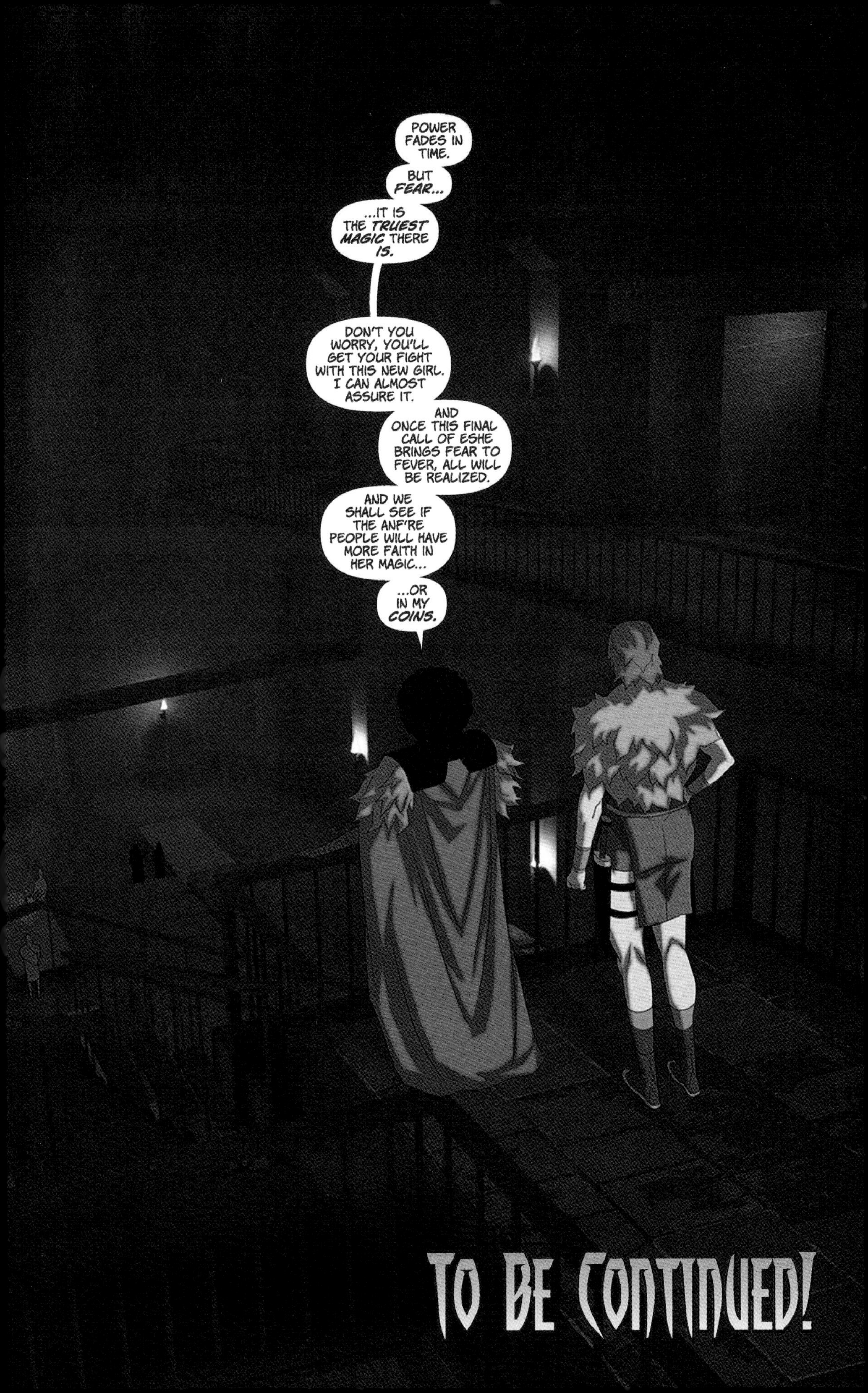
POWER FADES IN TIME.
BUT FEAR...
...IT IS THE TRUEST MAGIC THERE IS.
DON'T YOU WORRY, YOU'LL GET YOUR FIGHT WITH THIS NEW GIRL. I CAN ALMOST ASSURE IT.
AND ONCE THIS FINAL CALL OF ESHE BRINGS FEAR TO FEVER, ALL WILL BE REALIZED.
AND WE SHALL SEE IF THE ANF'RE PEOPLE WILL HAVE MORE FAITH IN HER MAGIC...
...OR IN MY COINS.
TO BE CONTINUED!

Esutela's Fables
The Horses and The Sheep
Hadi'esutelayami
Timvayaku Milheku

On a hill, a sheep without wool saw some horses,
NA GWEPE, TIMVANKAIKU MU TEI MILHEMOSAIBOKU WA,

one of them was pulling a heavy wagon,
OGAIRENGAM MPA HEI KU,

one carrying a big load,
CHEGWANCHE SAU HEI KU,

and one was carrying her master quickly.
PYURU LHONGUGANGU SAU HEI KU.

The sheep said to the horses:
TIMVAYAKU ORO MI MILHEKU:

"My heart pains me, seeing someone driving horses."
"MAU TATAN NE, TIMVAKU FE KARO SEMANGU BEI."

The horses said: "Listen, sheep, our
hearts pain us when we see this:
ORO MI TIMVARIKU: "AM MO FAI,
MILHEDE, MAU TATAN NEYA, MO TEI E BEI:

An Anf're, the master, makes the wool of the
sheep into a warm garment for herself.
PAI GWOMOCHIGAYE LA SAIBO ANFANGU GA, LHONGUNGU.

And the sheep has no wool."
EI, YA KA SAIBO MILHEMBAKU BEI."

Having heard this, the sheep fled into the plain.
MI MO FAI MILHEKU WA, NA GOJOKWE TE WUGWA KU.

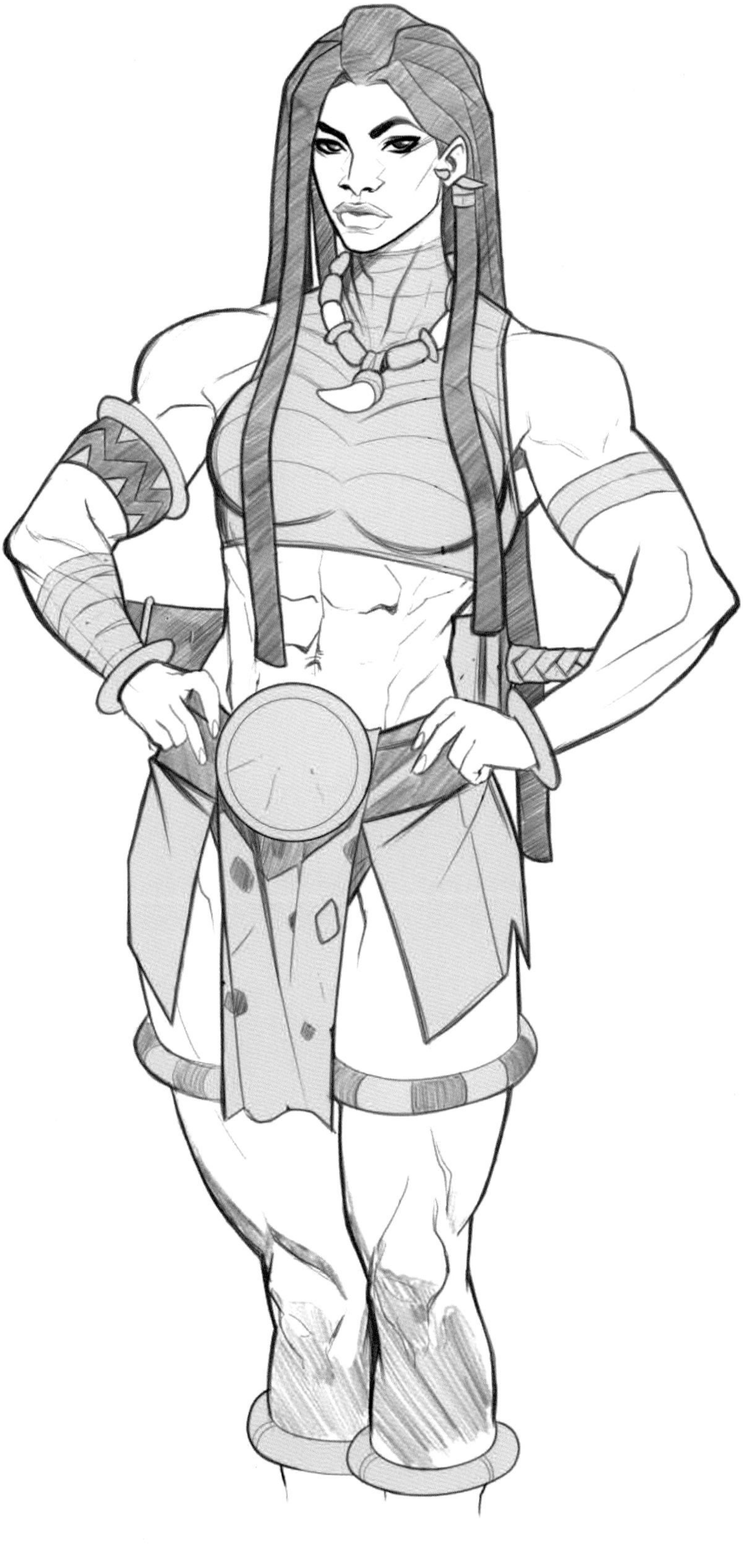

RECORDING
ARTIST RAPSODY
AND DEDREN SNEAD

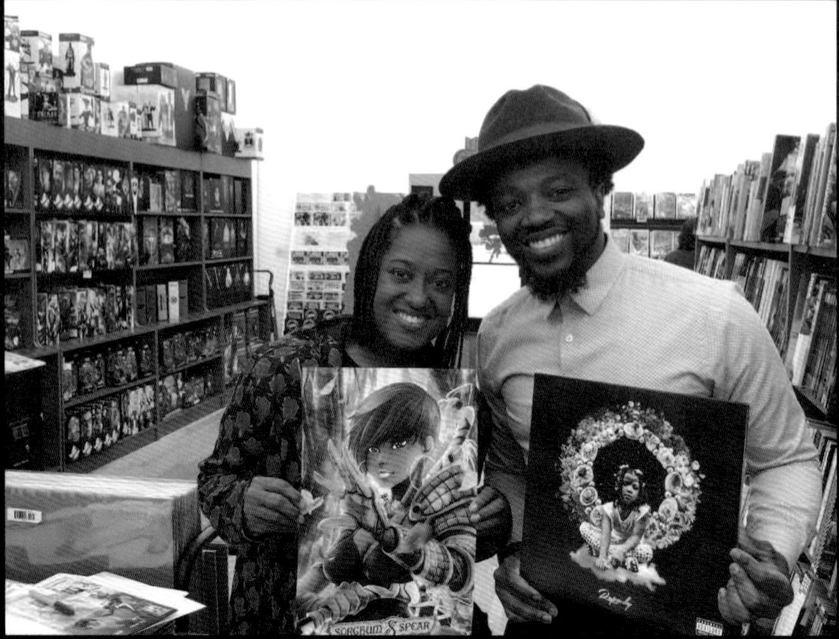
SORGHUM & SPEAR

ACTRESS NICHELLE NICHOLS
AND DEDREN SNEAD

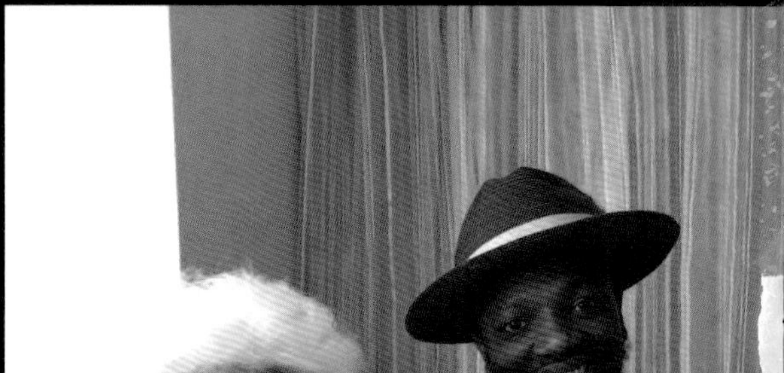

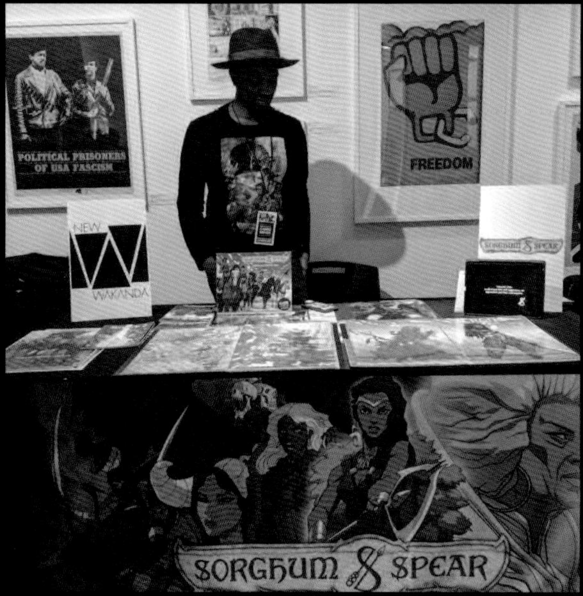
POLITICAL PRISONERS
OF USA FASCISM
FREEDOM
NEW
WAKANDA
SORGHUM & SPEAR

SORGHUM & SPEAR CREATOR
DEDREN SNEAD